Traveling History
With
Bonnie and Clyde

A Road Tripper's Guide
To Gangster Sites in Middle America

Robin Cole Jett

Traveling History with Bonnie and Clyde: A Road Tripper's Guide to Gangster Sites in Middle America
Copyright © 2008 by Robin Cole Jett

ISBN: 978-0-615-24103-6

Library of Congress Control Number: 2008907434

Manufactured in the United States of America

Red River Historian Press
101 Montego Bay Lewisville, TX 75067
972-353-4130

Visit *Red River Historian Press* at
http://www.redriverhistorian.com

Publisher's Cataloging-in-Publication

Cole-Jett, Robin.
    Traveling history with Bonnie and Clyde: a road tripper's guide to gangster sites in middle America / by Robin Cole Jett
        p. cm.
        Includes index and footnotes.
        LCCN: 2008907434
        ISBN: 9780615241036

Traveling History with Bonnie and Clyde

Table of Contents

Table of Photographs

24. Arlington Baptist College, formerly Top of the Hill Terrace, Arlington, Texas, author's collection.

25. Fort Worth Stockyards National Historic District, Fort Worth, Texas, author's collection.

26. Campus Theater, Denton, Texas, author's collection.

27. Ponder First State Bank, Ponder, Texas, author's collection.

28. Pano's Diner, Shreveport, Louisiana, author's collection.

29. Ambush site marker, Louisiana Hwy 154, near Gibsland, Louisiana, author's collection.

30. Floor of Conger Furniture Store, Arcadia, Louisiana, author's collection.

31. Road side fruit stand in Stringtown, Oklahoma, author's collection.

32. Stretch of Route 66 Ribbon Road, near Miami, Oklahoma, author's collection.

33. "Joplin Hideout," Joplin, Missouri, author's collection.

34. Interior of Jesse James House Museum, St. Joseph, Missouri, author's collection.

35. Neon sign, Dexter, Iowa, author's collection.

36. US Hwy 77 in Arbuckle Mountains, Oklahoma, author's collection.

37. Texas Tourist Camp cabin, Decatur, Texas, author's collection.

38. Pistol taken from dead Bonnie's lap, Texas Prison Museum, Huntsville, Texas, author's collection.

39. Texas Rangers Museum sign, Waco, Texas, author's collection.

40. Bridge over Salt Fork of the Red River, Wellington, Texas, author's collection.

Front and Back Covers: Raccoon River near Dexter, Iowa, author's collection; Bonnie Parker and Clyde Barrow, Hayes Collection, Dallas Public Library.

Acknowledgments

Many people have helped me create this book, whether they know it or not. I'd like to say "thank you" to David Jett, my son and traveling buddy, who has accompanied me on most of the road trips in this book; Raymond Jett, my husband and some-time traveling companion, who helped with computer issues and was an all-around supporter; June and Gordon Davis, my in-laws who would keep an eye on David when I needed it; Barbara and Leroy Baker, my parents who gave me support; Christy Cole, Andrew Dacus and Rebecca Dacus, my sister, nephew, and niece who were of great help; Ray Brister and Chris Rose, who took photos and helped me to laugh a lot; Lisa Martin, who edited this book with an eagle eye and accompanied me on one of the road trips; Patricia Feager, who read excerpts and offered me helpful criticism; and Ryan Cook, who taught me a lot about software and formatting.

Further, I'd like to thank those who've inspired me: Bill James, Barbara Winter, Mark Ortman, Frank Dobie, Angie Debo, Ph.D., T. Lindsay Baker, Ph.D., Katherine Landdeck, Ph.D., John Neal Phillips, and the writers of the Federal Works Project Administration, whose WPA Guides have been an invaluable source to me for all things that make America, America.

Introduction to the Book

I've been a road tripper since childhood. Some of my earliest and fondest memories involve climbing into the back seat of my dad's car, and together with my family, heading into the great wide open – or even just for a drive around the neighborhood. I never cared where we were headed, but enjoyed the comforting rhythm of the road noise just the same.

I never did understand how my sister could sleep on long trips. I would stare out onto the fields, prairies, railroad tracks, streams, and homes that whizzed by my window. Entranced, I'd imagine what lay just beyond the horizon. I made plans to one day find out where the goliath electric poles stretched to. I envisioned actually living out of my car and traveling where the wind took me.

As I grew older, I gradually discovered that aimless road tripping wasn't really doing it for me anymore. I wanted to know more about the things I was seeing. The storyteller in me was insatiably curious, so once I could drive myself anywhere I wanted, my road trips became more like expeditions in which I would try to learn why this town was founded, why that town died and this town prospered, what this ruin used to be, and what had happened in this landscape.

That's why I ended up studying history. Of all academic disciplines, history fed my curiosity and still left me hungry for more. Wedding history with my road tripping made my explorations that much more enjoyable.

So when I learned that Bonnie and Clyde had lived and died not too very far from where I grew up – in Paris, Texas and Shreveport, Louisiana – I decided to take some historical road trips based on their exploits. Over time, I amassed a collection of sorts, filled with information on the places they had visited, the sights they might have seen, and the roads that they had traveled. Surprisingly, many of these places still exist, and I gradually realized that other history buffs would enjoy retracing their steps, too.

I don't purport to be an authority on Bonnie and Clyde; this travel guide is more of a hybrid than a true history book. While I took great pains to be as accurate as possible in the brief retelling of their story, I was more concerned with their experiences on the road than with what kinds of guns they used or what they might have said. The purpose of this book is for you, a fellow road tripper, to get a feel for gangster-era America, and to be able to see things you'd normally not go out of your way to see.

Once one discovers the story behind the road, I've learned, the ordinary becomes enthralling. As a road tripper yourself, I'm sure you know exactly what I mean.

Happy Trails!

To the Victims

In history, there are always stories that go untold. Those who are downtrodden are usually not afforded the same historical place as those who stepped on them, and the conqueror leaves little room for the accounts of those he conquered. Though the nature of history has been slowly changing, most histories do tend to focus on the "bad" characters: people who lived larger than life, people whose reckless disregard for others placed them into the historical record.

In this short, historical travel guide, the murderers are given far more space than those they killed. While I use Bonnie Parker and Clyde Barrow's exploits as reference, in no way do I wish to disregard the men, all in their prime and all upstanding family men, who were murdered for no other reason except that they crossed paths with vicious people.

The famous Chicago journalist Mike Royko interviewed the children and widows of the Barrow Gang's murder victims upon the release of the 1967 movie, *Bonnie and Clyde*. The resulting article shed light on the reality of a violent death's aftermath. Jim Campbell, the son of Cal Campbell who was murdered in 1934, quit college when he became depressed, and he never did go back. Claude Harryman's life was put on hold when he had to provide for his siblings and mother after his father, Wes Harryman, was killed for merely serving a search warrant to the Barrow Gang in Joplin, Missouri. The family had to sell their farm and find work in the WPA.

Even more tragic are the circumstances under which most of these men died. Many were farmers, not professional lawmen. They had picked up jobs as deputy sheriffs and constables to get their families through the Depression, using their own hunting rifles as their only weapons. This was the time before Social Security, so when the main provider was killed, their families became destitute.

Following is a chronological list (by death date) of the murder victims, and their occupations at the time of their death.

In Memoriam

John Bucher (Hillsboro, TX, 1932) - Shopkeeper
Eugene Moore (Atoka, OK, 1932) - Police Officer
Howard Hall (Sherman, TX, 1932) - Shopkeeper/butcher
Doyle Johnson (Temple, TX, 1932) - Private Citizen
Malcolm Davis (Dallas, TX, 1933) - Sheriff's Deputy
Harry McGinnis (Joplin, MO, 1933) - Police Officer
Wes Harryman (Joplin, MO, 1933) - Police Officer
Henry Humphrey (Alma, AK, 1933) - Police Officer
Major Crowson (Huntsville, TX, 1934) - Prison Guard
E.B. Wheeler (Grapevine, TX, 1934) - Police Officer
H.D. Murphy (Grapevine, TX, 1934) - Police Officer
Cal Campbell (Commerce, OK, 1934) – Constable

A Historical Fascination

Few criminals in history have fascinated us as much as Bonnie Parker and Clyde Barrow. John Dillinger may have been Public Enemy Number One, and Jesse James may have been the all-American outlaw-hero. But Bonnie and Clyde, young, in love, and desperately in trouble, have stirred our imaginations for over eighty years, and we still can't turn away from their story.

Bonnie and Clyde lived in the proverbial "hard times" – their escapades in the Southwestern and Midwestern United States skirted the edge of the Dust Bowl. Coming from poor white families, both lived in the "Bog," a dilapidated and dangerous West Dallas neighborhood. Their situation made them true outcasts in a time when many people felt alienated from their environment and their government. In a strange way, Bonnie and Clyde embodied the "dirty thirties."

Their story also represented an era that we've only now come to appreciate. Clyde loved cars and used them as tools unlike any criminal has done before or since. He and Bonnie lived on the road, driving hundreds of miles in one day, perpetually on the run. They camped along the road, slept in people's driveways, stayed in simple road-side motels, and ate in down-home diners. In their many (stolen) cars, they turned their backs on the desolation of the Depression and sought out the wide vistas and open spaces not unlike the pioneers did two generations before them. Although they lived on borrowed time, that time seemed to afford them more freedom than what they could have expected had they lived normal lives.

The story of Bonnie and Clyde's crime spree would probably have remained regional lore had it not been for two brilliant story tellers. David Newman and Robert Benton wrote the script for the movie *Bonnie and Clyde,* which Arthur Penn directed and Warren Beatty produced (and starred in). That film, historians say, ushered in the new golden age of American cinema. In 1967, when the movie was released, viewers were repelled yet amazed by the violence of *Bonnie and Clyde.* The film forced its audience to sympathize with the criminals. The decidedly unhappy ending jolted viewers out of complacency and into a realistic and ugly world. With good reason, *Bonnie and Clyde* has been considered a hallmark of American theater.

Many more reasons and explanations abound as to why we remain interested in Bonnie and Clyde. The most interesting part of their story for anyone who likes to combine history and travel, however, is that one can still retrace the paths Bonnie and Clyde followed. A driving tour of their exploits leads one to forgotten roads, abandoned bridges, their gravestones, and old buildings that may whisper a story or two.

So come along as we follow Bonnie and Clyde throughout middle America. Starting in Dallas and ending in Louisiana, we will also visit Missouri, Iowa, and Oklahoma along the way. This guide will be your companion as you travel along the historic path that America's most infamous lovers forged.

A Short History of the Barrow Gang

Bonnie and Clyde's Dallas

In the roaring twenties, Dallas was brazenly young, eager, and prosperous. Built on business (and not always legal business), the city worked hard to be considered sophisticated, turning its back on its western past and embracing a future that looked eastward for inspiration. The citizens of Dallas were very aggressive in acquiring more power or prestige – for example, in the 1870s Dallas convinced the Texas and Pacific Railroad to headquarter in their town, though Jefferson, to the east, may have been a more strategic center. This progressive attitude began early with people like John Neely Bryan, the area's original land grant holder, who persuaded families to settle along the Trinity river bottoms even though the only building in the town at that time was Bryan's cabin.

Busy Akard Street in Dallas. Image courtesy of the Dallas Public Library.

Like many southern cities, Dallas was highly segregated in the twenties and thirties. Oak Cliff, which had been incorporated into Dallas in 1910, was a predominantly working class, white town on the south side of the Trinity. Little Mexico established itself just northwest of downtown, and Dallas' well-heeled Anglos lived along Gaston Avenue in East Dallas. Highland Park, which would become Dallas' toniest neighborhood – some call it "the Beverly Hills of Dallas" – had just been platted, and the Jewish enclave along Forest Avenue, where Stanley Marcus, founder of Nieman Marcus, grew up, was tight-knit and prosperous.

African Americans lived in pocket neighborhoods to the north and east of downtown. Most of their neighborhoods abutted the many train tracks that zig-zagged across the city. Deep Ellum, which today hosts funky clubs, bars, and tattoo parlors, was a freedman's town that was bordered to the east by the Texas and Pacific Railroad. The tracks of the Houston Texas Central and Missouri-Kansas- Texas railroads cut swaths right through the State-Thomas freedman's town in North Dallas.

This racially and economically segregated city molded criminals, artists, and business people alike. An eclectic and often eccentric mix of people from all over the United Sates and the world converged on this booming city to make it one of Texas' largest and history's most interesting.

Poor whites, who flocked to the city to escape sharecropping, found their way to West Dallas – the Bog. Anchored by a cement plant and remnants of the La Reunion and Eagle Ford settlements (and, by 1936, a lead smelter), the Bog had always been a sore spot for Dallas. It had been the area's red light district before the Civil War, and as more poor white sharecroppers arrived from the countryside to find their luck in the city, the Bog became a residential slum area. The low, unpainted shacks that lined the unpaved streets did not have sewage systems, and residents were often flooded out of their homes by the unpredictable Trinity River.[1] Also known as the Devil's Back Porch, this neglected, unincorporated neighborhood became home to some of Texas' most notorious criminals, two of which were Bonnie and Clyde.[2]

West Dallas became home to the Barrows and Parkers. Image courtesy of the Dallas Public Library.

The Barrows Come to Dallas

Clyde Barrow was born on March 24, 1909, the fourth of eight children, to Henry and Cumie Barrow from Telico Plains, Ellis County. The Barrows were poor sharecroppers and often farmed out their children to wealthier relatives. Clyde was an active, unruly child. He disliked school – and any kind of structure, apparently. Though the family had a lot of struggles, they were close, plain spoken, and protective of their own.

Like many farmers, by the early 1920s the Barrows had had enough of eking out a living from their meager plot of land, and they moved to Dallas to start their lives anew. At first, the family lived alongside the Trinity River bottoms in a free camp ground beneath the Houston Street Viaduct. Thereafter, they lived for a short while with daughter Nell, who had married Luther Cowan. Cowan turned out to be one of the few positive influences in Clyde's life – he taught Clyde to play the saxophone.[3]

Clyde quit school in 7th grade and, with his brothers L.C. and Buck, helped his father gather scrap metal to sell. The scrap they gathered may have not necessarily been thrown away – Clyde's first crimes probably involved stealing copper tubing. Henry Barrow drove a mule team across the viaducts to ferry the scrap, and after his team was hit and killed by a car, Henry opened a service station with the settlement money. Selling Texaco gas at the Star Service Station on Eagle Ford Road, Henry attached a little shack to the station to house his family.[4]

Clyde Barrow, possibly somewhere in East Texas, during his short but serious crime spree. Image courtesy of the Dallas Public Library.

Clyde first gained a reputation with the law because of a woman. While working at A&K Auto Top Works in Dallas, he fell in love with Eleanor Williams. Though she lived in the classy Forest Avenue area, her parents seemed to have liked Clyde. Clyde and Eleanor were contemplating marriage and he even had her initials tattooed on his arm.[5]

After a fight with Clyde, Eleanor escaped to visit family in Broddus, a small town near San Augustine, Texas. When Clyde's impatient nature got the better of him, he rented a car to drive down to Broddus and work out their differences. Clyde didn't return the car on time, so the rental company called the police. Instead of explaining why the car rental was overdue, Clyde ran away. Eleanor's parents found that behavior just a tad suspicious and forced her to break up with Clyde.

Considering Clyde's upbringing, running away from a uniformed officer may have not been so surprising. Because West Dallas was so crime ridden, police officers only patrolled in pairs. Clyde and his brothers were harassed regularly by the police, just like most of the young men from the neighborhood. Clyde had trouble keeping jobs because of this.

In 1929, Clyde and his brother Buck decided to give the police a reason to harass them. They graduated from stealing chickens to breaking into a service station in Denton and trying to lug its safe back to Dallas. During that job, Clyde escaped from the police, but his brother was arrested and sentenced to five years in prison. Buck's wife divorced him soon after, and Buck escaped from prison a few months later.[6]

Clyde still went out to commit crimes around Waco and Henderson, Texas. For the most part, however, Clyde hid out in the West Dallas neighborhood he knew so well, ducking whenever he saw the police, until he met up with a tiny, sprite young woman named Bonnie.

The Parkers Come to Dallas

Born in Rowena, Runnels County, on October 1, 1910, Bonnie was the middle child of Emma and Charles Parker. She, her parents, and her siblings, Billie and Buster, lived in a modest yet comfortable home in the little west Texas town where Charles Parker worked as a bricklayer. After Charles suddenly died, Emma moved her family to her mother's house in Cement City, a company town on the edge of West Dallas.[7]

Cement City was dusty, dirty, and choked with pollution. Most of the men in Cement City had run-ins with the law because they had difficulty finding work. Emma found work herself as a seamstress, and often put in ten-hour days while her kids ran the streets.

Bonnie in a studio portrait. Apparently, she followed the fashion of the day, and was quite the make-up aficionado. Image courtesy of the Dallas Public Library.

Unlike her future lover, Bonnie enjoyed school and her teachers enjoyed her. Bonnie liked to be the center of attention and willingly read her poetry to anyone who'd listen. Her grades were always above average – she was considered a "star pupil."[8] Gang members described her as very funny, self-deprecating, and a bit of a romantic.[9] She apparently had a big heart, especially for children, and enjoyed writing poetry. According to Clyde's sister-in-law, Blanche Barrow, she later developed a drinking problem.[10]

Even in high school, Bonnie tended to hang out with the tougher crowd. In this group of friends she met her husband, Roy Thornton, a small-time West Dallas hood. Bonnie was only sixteen when they married. Roy made it clear very early that he liked to be with his friends and their criminal activities more than with her and left her for months at a time.[11] Being in and out of jail while leaving her with no money, Bonnie essentially lived the life of a single, working girl. Though she and Roy had a place of their own, she would often visit her mother to ease her loneliness.

After marriage, Bonnie worked as a waitress in several cafes in downtown Dallas. At one point, she waited tables at the Marcos Café next to the courthouse, where she bantered with several of the men who years later would have a hand in killing her, such as Bob Alcorn and Sheriff Smoot Schmidt.[12] Another one of these men was Ted Hinton, a sheriff's deputy who also grew up along the mean streets of West Dallas. In his memoirs, Hinton recalled being the only person that the Barrows could trust (insofar as a criminal's family can trust law enforcement) after Clyde ran afoul of the law.[13]

Bonnie stopped working at the café around 1929. To cut living expenses and earn a little money, she moved in with a friend who had broken her arm and needed some household help. As fate would have it, Clyde paid a visit to the same house to hang out with Clarence Clay, Bonnie's friend's father.[14] When Bonnie and Clyde met, there seemed to have been an instant, intense, and mutual attraction – Clyde dumped his present girlfriend after meeting Bonnie, and Bonnie forgot all about being Mrs. Roy Thornton.

Clyde's Graduation to Serious Crime

Bonnie and Clyde quickly became a committed couple, and Clyde spent a lot of time at Bonnie's mother's house. It was there that in 1930, Clyde was arrested for burglary and sent to the McLennan County jail in Waco. While Emma Parker immediately pointed out to Bonnie that this was a bad sign – she probably used bad ol' Roy Thornton as a perfect example of Bonnie's poor choice in men - Bonnie wouldn't hear of it. Instead, she hitched a ride with Cumie Barrow to visit Clyde in jail. She wrote many letters to Clyde, imploring him to "do good" once he got out of prison.[15]

During one of her visits, Clyde persuaded Bonnie to break into a fellow inmate's relative's house, where she would find a gun. He asked her to bring him the weapon so that he could spring from jail. Along with her cousin, with whom she stayed in Waco, Bonnie broke into the house, retrieved the gun, and smuggled it into Clyde's jail cell. Clyde and the inmate escaped that same day. Bonnie left for Dallas and waited in vain for Clyde to call on her at her mother's house. Feeling used, her anger subsided when she received a letter from Clyde, who wrote that he was trying to find a job in Middleton, Ohio. His plan didn't work out because he was caught and sent to the Eastham Prison Farm near Huntsville, Texas.[16]

Huntsville was the seat of the Texas prison system and home to death row. The infamous Walls Unit, a red brick fortress which dominated the city, housed the most hardened criminals. Just northeast of the Walls Unit was the notorious prison farm Eastham, where offenders planted crops, broke rock, harvested cotton, and dug irrigation ditches for area landowners. This form of "indentured servitude," for want of a better term, was a boon for the state, as it displayed the prison's self-sufficiency and Texas' "tough on crime" stance. For the prisoners, however, Eastham served as a poor man's hell on earth. Beatings, torture, and malnourishment were not uncommon.[17]

Clyde was among those who experienced Eastham's reputation first hand. Beaten and possibly sodomized by a building tender named "Big Ed," Clyde struck him with a pipe and killed him. Though another inmate took the blame, the prison never investigated the matter. Clyde thus got away with his first (though probably justified) murder. While working in back-breaking labor for twelve hours a day, he met several men who would form his gang, including Ralph Fults, Joe Palmer, and Henry Methvin.[18]

Clyde learned through the grapevine that his brother Buck was coming to the Walls Unit to turn himself in as a favor to his new wife, Blanche. Blanche Caldwell was a pretty divorcee from Oklahoma who had fallen madly in love with Buck and wanted him to start their new life together with a clean slate. Because Buck was voluntarily returning to prison (after he had escaped and been on the run for several months), he probably would not be sent to Eastham – so in order for Clyde to be near his brother, Clyde would have to leave the farm. Clyde persuaded another inmate to chop off two of his toes, which would bring him to the infirmary at the Walls Unit. In the kind of tragic-comedy that defined Clyde's life, he was paroled two weeks later. His mother Cumie had been working for over a year to get his fourteen year sentence reduced, and she had succeeded.[19]

In February of 1932, Clyde returned to Dallas and immediately sought out Bonnie, who, though she had been writing him letters while he was in prison, had dated other men in the interim. Like his brother Buck did for Blanche, Clyde tried to "go straight" for Bonnie's sake. He took a number of jobs but was often harassed by the police, who either accused him of crimes or questioned him about his family and friends. Gradually, Clyde began to realize that his reputation preceded him. He couldn't keep a job, and memories of Eastham had apparently hardened him. Prior to his stiff sentence, he had been a trouble maker, but not necessarily a violent one. The never-ending labor, humiliations, and deplorable working conditions at Eastham, experienced day in and day out under the threat of gunfire, made him angry, violent, and calculating. Gang member Ralph Fults likened him to a "rattlesnake."[20]

The Barrow Gang Forms

In the spring of 1932 Clyde formed the first incarnation of the Barrow Gang. The original members included Raymond Hamilton and Ralph Fults. Raymond was a West Dallas kid who, together with his brother Floyd, stole cars and sold them as scrap. He was no stranger to jail, having been a frequent guest because he wasn't a very competent criminal. By the time he was ten, Raymond had been in trouble with the law for truancy, vagrancy, and vandalism. For all his faults, however, Raymond was not a violent man. Abandoned by his father, he doted on his mother, who experienced more than her fair share of heartache from her boys.[21]

Ralph Fults was the son of a McKinney, Texas, farmer who met Clyde at Eastham, where Ralph was incarcerated for car theft and prison breaks. Ralph was instrumental (literally) in getting Raymond to join the gang after he brought a hacksaw to

Raymond Hamilton

Dapper Raymond Hamilton, Clyde's BFF for a while. Image courtesy of the Dallas Public Library.

Raymond's jail cell in McKinney. Clyde became close friends with Ralph while in prison. According to Ralph, it was while watching Ralph get pistol whipped by guards that Clyde swore revenge on Eastham. [22]

In his book, *Running with Bonnie and Clyde: The Ten Fast Years of Ralph Fults*, John Neal Phillips explains that staging a raid on Eastham became Clyde's mission in life. Clyde's ultimate goal, according to Phillips, was to accumulate enough money, weapons, and men to help others break out of Eastham.

The new gang roamed haphazardly across the countryside, robbing banks and factories' payrolls, but for the most part they came up empty handed. This was during the height of the Great Depression, and banks were closing to the tune of 3,000 a year.[23]

With little money and no real prospects, Raymond ended up leaving Clyde for a time. John Neal Phillips writes that Raymond left because he had heard about Clyde's plan for the prison raid and wanted no part in it. Instead, Raymond formed his own band with his brother and associates from Wichita Falls, but would remain close to Clyde and accompany him on later criminal endeavors.[24] Clyde and Ralph continued to drive around, hoping to find recruits for their fledgling gang. They went as far as Amarillo to meet up with people who, they were told, were interested in joining. During the trip back to Dallas from Amarillo, Clyde committed his first of several kidnappings – in fact, Clyde would gain notoriety for his weird hostage taking. In Electra, a small town just south of Vernon, Texas, and named after a daughter of the Waggoner ranchers, Clyde and Ralph kidnapped Chief of Police James T. Taylor and A. F. McCormick, an oil and gas field agent. They stole McCormick's car and, after an eight mile ride, let their unwilling passengers go. When they ran out of gas, Clyde and Ralph commandeered W.N. Owens' car. After riding around with Owens, the pair let him out in Oklahoma.[25]

Bonnie Gets in Trouble

Bonnie had been waiting patiently on Clyde's return from his many exploits. Because she had not suffered any repercussions when she smuggled a gun into the Waco jail, Bonnie felt it was time to let her in on the crimes now, too. Clyde, Ralph, and Bonnie drove to Kemp, a small town in Kaufman County, to break into the Robert H. Brock store to steal guns and ammo.

While they labored to open the door of the store, David Brennan, the Mabank Chief of Police, caught sight of the trio. He sounded the town's alarm, which brought dozens of people out of their beds. With this crowd watching, Clyde, Bonnie, and Ralph jumped into their car and careened back and forth through town, looking for an escape. As they headed down a country road, they got mired in the black gumbo mud the North Texas region is (in)famous for. Ditching the car, they jumped on mules they found in a pasture, but the animals balked. They then stole another car, but it too got stuck in the mud. They hid in the brush for the rest of the day, as everyone in the county, including everyone's dogs, searched for them. When they were found, Clyde fired a few shots at two police officers, then ran between them as they reloaded, leaving Bonnie and Ralph behind.[26]

Ralph and Bonnie, who called themselves Jack Sherman and Betty Thornton once apprehended, were taken to the town's calaboose to wait for removal to the county jail the next day. Ralph had been shot in the short altercation, but did not receive any medical attention. Bonnie smoked "cigarette after cigarette," as the newspaper reported. She supposedly hissed at the many eyes watching her through the iron bars of the cinder-block hoosegow.[27]

To spare Bonnie and Clyde (even though Clyde had abandoned them), Ralph took the blame for the attempted robbery. After a stay in Wichita Falls, he was transferred to Huntsville, where he became friends with Buck Barrow.[28]

Bonnie remained in the Kaufman County jail for several weeks. Her mother, who befriended the warden's wife, probably wanted to keep her there to make her come to her senses. Cumie and Blanche Barrow also visited her.[29] While languishing in prison, Bonnie penned a poem that alarmed her mother with its graphic details and gangster-style wording: "The Story of Suicide Sal."[30]

After being no-billed by a grand jury, Bonnie returned to her mother's home in West Dallas. Bonnie felt betrayed by Clyde and told her family and friends that their relationship was over.[31]

Murders for Real – 1932

Clyde used the time while Bonnie languished in jail very unwisely. He caught up with Raymond Hamilton again, and together with a number of men who were in and out of their gang, they committed other robberies around North Texas and established hideouts in Grand Prairie and around Lake Dallas.[32] During a robbery of a wayside store in Hillsboro, Clyde and the others met with resistance – and Ted Rogers, one of the members, shot and killed the storekeeper, John Bucher. Raymond Hamilton, still just a small-time West Dallas thug and car thief, was pinned for the crime.[33] Clyde Barrow escaped suspicion – for now.

But 1932 was a bloody year for the Southwest, thanks to Clyde and his entourage. The Barrow Gang never deliberately set out to kill anyone (with one exception in 1934), but Clyde's temper could get the better of him, and the inexperience in the gang with weapons (and crime, of course) often caused unwarranted tragedy.

Three murders cemented Clyde's reputation as a vicious and dangerous criminal. In the parking lot of a dance hall in Stringtown, Oklahoma, Clyde, Raymond, and Everett Mulligan, a friend from West Dallas, were approached by Sheriff C.G. Maxwell and Deputy E.C. Moore, who either were investigating alleged moonshine in the car, or needed help to get their own car out of a muddy rut (accounts differ). Without warning, Clyde and Raymond shot Moore dead and severely wounded Maxwell.

A few months later, Clyde supposedly robbed a grocery store in Sherman, Texas, and killed the butcher, Howard Hall.[34] A car theft in Temple, Texas, resulted in the murder of Doyle Johnson, who was either shot by Clyde or the newest gang member, W.D. (William Decaon) Jones.

Young W.D. Jones became a permanent third member of the Barrow Gang, though upon capture he claimed he had been kidnapped. Image courtesy of the Dallas Public Library.

Bonnie and Clyde

Bonnie sulked at home after her stint in jail. Although she felt betrayed by Clyde, she heeded his call as soon as he gave it and left home for good in July of 1932.[35] She lied and engaged in crime, rather than leave his side - after the murder in Stringtown, for example, she, Clyde and Raymond hid out in at Bonnie's aunt's house in Carlsbad, New Mexico. There, they kidnapped an officer when he came to check on them.

She and Clyde immediately formed a strong partnership and became inseparable. Clyde learned that she was the only person he could trust, and Bonnie figured out that Clyde accepted her just as she was.

Their love was strange but apparently genuine. Bonnie deferred to Clyde in all decisions and aided him when she could, making her a perfect partner. Why Bonnie remained attracted to a domineering criminal who took her away from her family, made her sleep in cars for months at a time, and put her in compromising situations, is anybody's guess. One can argue that she was an abused woman who could not leave her tormentor. On the other hand, she may have been a person who liked to live on edge, with all the excitement of danger and the promise of adventure. Her life before Clyde had held no real meaning, and she probably feared turning into her mother – old and bitter from worry and overwork. Life with Clyde offered an alternative, and she grasped it.

In an interview for *Playboy Magazine* the year the movie debuted, former gang member W.D. Jones recalled Bonnie as a fun-loving woman, a bit apathetic but with some genuine moments of self-inflection and self-deprecation. Blanche Barrow, Clyde's sister-in-law, described Bonnie as overly dramatic and a heavy drinker. Quite possibly, Bonnie was a dreamer. She glamorized her life with Clyde in her poetry and imagined herself in the crime magazines that she enjoyed reading. To Bonnie, the dangerous life on the road may have seemed romantic. In Clyde she found a person who shared her fatalism, her background, and fed her fantasies. Whatever the chemistry, those who knew them well declared that Bonnie and Clyde had been made for each other.

A rare closeness described Bonnie and Clyde's relationship. They used pet names, such as "sugar" for him and "baby" for her. Gang members treated Bonnie like a sister, but were cautious never to be too rude or familiar with her, as they saw Clyde as their boss. Former gang and family members also mentioned that Clyde had tried to convince Bonnie to surrender numerous times, but she refused to listen, of course. And while the movie version of their lives depicted Clyde as impotent, gang members repeatedly stated that he had no problem in the romance department.

With three murders, several robberies, and countless car thefts under his belt, Clyde – with Bonnie in tow – started to gain a reputation. People in West Dallas either thought of them as semi-heroes or bumbling idiots. As newspapers started to report

Clyde liked to share, and let Bonnie hold his guns. Image courtesy of the Dallas Public Library.

on Bonnie and Clyde, the American public became fascinated and fearful of these young kids who could outrun the law with a devil-may-care attitude. They epitomized the "escape" many people in the dark days of the Great Depression fantasized about. What kept Bonnie and Clyde on the run so long was not necessarily talent. Though Clyde was a good driver, he was aided by outdated laws in which police and sheriff officers could not cross county lines, let alone state lines, to chase suspects. He drove with a police radio,[36] and he also cut telephone wires when leaving town.[37] The law enforcement officers the pair encountered were mainly under-armed, under-trained, and under-paid. Their decrepit cars and shotguns could never measure up to Clyde's penchant for driving fast, eight cylinder cars and his retooled guns. Clyde modified his guns, which he stole from National Guard Armories in Texas, Louisiana, and Oklahoma, by welding several ammo clips together. This resulted in increased fire power but diminished control, with the result that the bullets dispersed helter-skelter. Clyde called his invention a "scatter gun."[38]

Red Light Murder, 1933

At the beginning of 1933, Clyde, Bonnie, and W.D. Jones renewed their search for more gang members. On the night of January 6, Clyde attempted to contact Floyd Hamilton, Raymond's brother. Clyde was wanting to recruit Floyd to help him spring Raymond from the Hillsboro prison, where he was being held for the murder of John Bucher of Hillsboro. Clyde knew that the West Dallas home of Lillian McBride, Floyd's and Raymond's sister, served as a meeting point for various characters of the West Dallas underworld, and he hoped to meet Floyd there.

However, Tarrant County sheriff deputies had been staking out the McBride house all day. They were hoping to catch Floyd and Odell Chambless, whom they believed had robbed the Grapevine Bank. Clyde asked Maggie Farris, another Hamilton sister who lived at the McBride home with her young children, to leave a red light in the window facing the street that night. If the light was extinguished, it would be a sign that the "laws" (as the gang called them) were away from the house, and Clyde could safely enter.

The officers had other plans. They commandeered the McBride home to await Floyd and Odell Chambless. When one of the officers ordered Maggie to turn off the red light, she yelled, "Don't shoot, think of my children" as Clyde, believing he was given the "all clear," rapped on the front door. As soon as Deputy Malcolm Davis opened the door, Clyde shot him, then fled to his car where Bonnie and W.D. Jones were waiting. Davis died at the scene, leaving all of Dallas reeling with the thought of a Barrow murder occurring so close to home.[39]

Family Reunion

After the Davis murder, Bonnie and Clyde decided that West Dallas wasn't a safe haven anymore. Together with W.D. Jones, his newly pardoned brother Buck Barrow, and Buck's wife Blanche, they rented a garage apartment in Joplin, Missouri, hoping to lie low for a while.

Blanche was not keen on staying with her wayward brother-in-law. Together with Cumie Barrow, she had worked hard on securing a pardon for Buck and hoped to start a new, clean life with the man whom she claimed was the love of her life. Buck promised Blanche that he would visit Clyde to talk him into going straight, though he knew in reality that would be a fruitless endeavor.[40] More likely, Buck met up with Clyde to get in on the action.

Though Blanche was a preacher's daughter, she stood by her man even as she noticed he was descending back into a life of crime. In the little apartment in Joplin, she tried her hardest to get along with Bonnie and turned a blind eye when Buck went out with W.D. to steal groceries and rob area gas stations. During the few weeks the gang lived in the apartment, the women rarely ventured out, and the men used the garages below to hide their arsenal of weapons. They also parked their cars facing the garage doors in order to make a clean get-away, should the need arise.[41]

That need came rather suddenly on April thirteenth. Local police had come to execute a warrant, under the suspicion that the residents of the garage apartment on 34th Street were bootleggers.[42] Neighbors had grown weary of the secretive young men and rarely seen women and reported their strange ways to the authorities.

Clyde, W.D., and Buck quickly engaged the police in a gun battle, in which Constable Wes Harryman and Detective Harry McGinnis were killed. During the chaos, Blanche ran out of the apartment after her dog, which startled the police. Apparently she was still running at a fast pace when she was picked up by the gang after they busted out of the garage with their car and escaped the volley of gun fire.[43]

A mug shot of Blanche Caldwell Barrow, a rather harried looking woman. Image courtesy of the Dallas Public Library.

They did not, however, escape scrutiny. Upon searching the apartment, Joplin police found items that cemented the legend of Bonnie and Clyde. They discovered rolls of film taken by Blanche, an avid photographer. Among these photos was the famous "cigar moll" pose, in which Bonnie wielded a weapon with a cigar clenched in her teeth. Other photos clearly depicted the pair and W.D. Jones in various ways: clowning around with guns, shooting at road signs, and proudly posing in front of their stolen cars. The police also found Buck's and Blanches' marriage certificate, Buck's pardon papers, and a tablet filled with Bonnie's poetry, most notably *The Story of Suicide Sal*. This well-written, though not terribly sophisticated, poem, which Bonnie had written while jailed in Kaufman, revealed Bonnie's romanticism and fatalism.

We each of us have a good "alibi"
For being down here in the "joint,"
But few of them really are justified
If you get right down to the point.

You've heard of a woman's glory
Being spent on a "downright cur,"
Still you can't always judge the story
As true, being told by her.

As long as I've stayed on this "island,"
And heard "confidence tales" from each "gal,"
Only one seemed interesting and truthful –
The story of "Suicide Sal."

Now "Sal" was a gal of rare beauty,
Though her features were coarse and tough
She never once faltered from duty
To play on the "up and up."

"Sal" told me this tale on the evening
Before she was turned out "free,"
And I'll do my best to relate it
Just as she told it to me:

I was born on a ranch in Wyoming
Not treated like Helen of Troy
I was taught that "rods were rulers"
And "ranked" as a greasy cowboy.

Then I left my old home for the city
To play in its mad dizzy whirl,
Not knowing how little of pity
It holds for a country girl.

There I fell for "the line" of a "henchman,"
A "professional killer" from "Chi,"
I couldn't help loving him madly
For him even now I would die.

One year we were desperately happy
Our "ill gotten gains" we spent free
I was taught the ways of the "underworld"
Jack was just like a "god" to me.

I got on the "F.B.A." payroll
To get the "inside lay" of the "job,"
The bank was "turning big money!"
It looked like a "cinch" for the "mob."

Eighty grand without even a "rumble" –
Jack was last with the "loot" in the door,
When the "teller" dead-aimed a revolver
From where they forced him to lie on the floor,

I knew I had only a moment –
He would surely get Jack as he ran;
So I "staged" a "big fade out" beside him
And knocked the forty-five out of his hand.

They "rapped me down big" at the station,
And informed me that I'd get the blame
For the "dramatic stunt" pulled on the "teller"
Looked to them too much like a "game."

The "police" called it a "frame-up,"
Said it was an "inside job,"
But I steadily denied any knowledge

On dealings with "underworld mobs."

The "gang" hired a couple of lawyers,
The best "fixers" in any man's town,
But it takes more than lawyers and money
When Uncle Sam starts "shaking you down."

I was charged as a "scion of gangland"
And tried for my wages of sin;
The "dirty dozen" found me guilty –
From five to fifty years in the pen.

I took the "rap" like good people,
And never one "squawk" I did make.
Jack "dropped himself" on the promise
That we make a "sensational break."

Well, to shorten a sad lengthy story,
Five years have gone over my head.
Without even so much as a letter –
At first I thought he was dead.

But not long ago I discovered
From a gal in the joint named Lyle,
That Jack and his "moll" had "got over,"
And were living in true "gangster style."

If he had returned to me sometime,
Though he hadn't a cent to give,
I'd forget all the hell he has caused me,
And love him as long as I live.

But there's no chance of his ever coming,
For he and his moll have no fears
But that I will die in this prison,
Or "flatten" this fifty years.

Tomorrow I'll be on the "outside"

And I'll "drop myself" on it today:
I'll "bump 'em" if they give me the "hotsquat,"
On this island out here in the bay...

The iron doors swung wide this morning
For a gruesome woman of waste,
Who at last had a chance to "fix it."
Murder showed in her cynical face.

Not long ago I read in the paper
That a gal on the East Side got "hot,"
And when the smoke finally retreated,
Two of gangdom were found "on the spot."

It related the colorful story
Of a "jilted gangster gal."
Two days later, a sub-gun ended
The story of "Suicide Sal."[44]

Driving into the Salt Fork

After the shootout in Missouri, the gang drove south to
Ruston, Louisiana, where they stole a car and took the owner and
his girlfriend hostage. Like most of their other kidnappings, they
released the couple unharmed after a drive of several hundred
miles. Thereafter, the group split up: Buck and Blanche stole a
car in order to take a holiday to Florida, and Clyde, Bonnie, and
W.D. roamed the southwest.[45] They planned to meet up in
Oklahoma in a few weeks' time.

On their way to the rendezvous point in western
Oklahoma, Clyde ignored a sign warning that the bridge over the
Salt Fork of the Red River, just north of Wellington, Texas, was
out. Driving at top speed, his car plunged several feet into the
river bottoms. Clyde and W.D. were thrown clear of the car, but
Bonnie was pinned. She screamed in pain as fire leapt around
her. As W.D. picked up the guns that had been scattered
everywhere after the fall, Clyde pulled Bonnie from the
wreckage.[46]

The Pritchard family, who owned a nearby farm, had witnessed the entire event from their front porch. They raced to help the outlaws. Clyde carried Bonnie into the house, whose "face [was] blistered, arms [were] seared" and "her leg [was] a mass of cooked flesh," as Emma Parker would describe it later.[47] Mrs. Pritchard rubbed bicarbonate of soda onto Bonnie's burns, which possibly saved her life.[48]

The farmers who had gathered at the Pritchard house after the crash became suspicious of the gang – not only did the guns make them wonder, but Clyde's outright refusal to bring Bonnie to a doctor seemed mighty suspicious. A neighboring farmer, Lonzo Carter, notified the sheriff. When Clyde saw Sheriff George Corry and City Marshall Paul Hardy pull up to the house, he and W.D. shot at them, in the process shooting the fingers of one of the Pritchard's daughters. They then took the men hostage, stole the sheriff's car, and drove to Oklahoma with Bonnie who, fading in and out of consciousness, lay across the kidnapped men's laps. They met Buck and Blanche near Erick, Oklahoma. Buck tied the officers to a tree using barbed wire. [49]

The Tourist Camps

Clyde drove the gang to the Twin Cities Tourist Camp in Fort Smith, Arkansas, where he hoped he could lie low and tend to Bonnie's wounds. With Bonnie, Blanche, Buck, and W.D. Jones squared away, Clyde drove down to Dallas to pick up Billie, Bonnie's sister. Together with Blanche, Billie nursed Bonnie as best she could.[50] Clyde stole a doctors' bag in order to get supplies. Some historical accounts maintain that Clyde chose to hide out at Fort Smith because a doctor connected to the underworld lived in the vicinity, who may have previously treated Pretty Boy Floyd.[51]

Blanche recalled how distraught Clyde was over Bonnie's ailment. He even carried her to the bathroom. Bonnie herself was mostly delusional from pain, and often tried to punch Blanche. According to Blanche, Bonnie was a horrible patient who complained loudly and was completely ungrateful.[52] Escaping the drama, W.D. and Buck roamed the countryside to find money for the gang. After robbing a Piggly Wiggly, Buck shot and killed Alma (Arkansas) City Marshall Henry Humphrey in a gunfight. They were also accused of assaulting a woman, though that story never panned out.[53]

Clyde sent Billie back to Texas and drove north to Oklahoma, where he gathered a new stockpile of weapons at the National Guard armory in Enid. He then rented two rooms at the Red Crown Tourist Camp in Platte City, Missouri, to hide out once again.[54]

The gang immediately aroused curiosity in the little town. Blanche, under Clyde's directions, rented the rooms and bought take-out dinners, but with small change. Blanche shopped at different pharmacies, buying potent medical supplies like syringes and atropine sulphate (a secretions inhibitor) to tend to Bonnie's wounds.[55]

Yet again, there was no rest for the gang. Local law enforcement had become suspicious and, upon realizing who they were dealing with, surrounded the cabin. In the middle of the night, officers knocked on Buck's and Blanche's door, ordering them to come out. Blanche called out, "Just a minute, let us get dressed," then, "They're in the other cabin." That's when Clyde and W.D. opened fire from the other cabin.[56]

Though a barrage of bullets rained down on the gang, they got away – even Bonnie with her wounds was surprisingly agile. This time, however, they had collateral damage. Buck was gravely injured with a shot to the head, and pieces of glass from the shot car window cut Blanche's eyes.[57]

Clyde and W.D. drove all night listening to the rest of the gang wailing. The car must have been disastrous inside, with the smell of gunpowder, blood and medicine mingling with the pleas of both women to stop the car. Buck was delirious. His wound was large, though not instantly fatal: his skull had been cracked, but the bullet had not lodged into his head.

Dexter, Iowa

Clyde found an abandoned amusement park in Dexter, Iowa, to set up camp. They resigned themselves to living out in the open for a while, under a canopy of trees. Clyde visited the little town to get supplies, careful not to be seen too often. He poured hydrogen peroxide into Buck's open wound, which may have helped to prolong his life, though Emma Parker said that doctors had told her that that was "the worst thing possible."[58]

Dexter, a small farming community reeling from the Great Depression, was also a close-knit place where everyone knew each other's business. Clyde aroused suspicion just by being a stranger in town, and no doubt a dirty one, considering he hadn't had much opportunity for a good bath or a visit to the washeteria. To keep the gang from going hungry, he had to buy take-out food. In the 1930s, getting take-out required bringing the silver ware and dishes back to the restaurant, preferably clean. Since Clyde could not do that, he garnered even more scrutiny.[59]

A local farmer notified the sheriff that he had found a pile of bloody bandages that had been burned on his land, and more people began reporting strange activity in the area. Law enforcement had already been on high alert to watch out for the Barrow Gang, because newspapers around the country had reported their exploits, and they were known to be armed and extremely dangerous. The laws finally realized that knocking on doors to execute search warrants was not the best way to deal with this gang, thus an ambush was planned on the group's campsite.

After hearing that the sheriff was going to attack the group, many of the more nosier citizens came out to watch. On the morning of July 24, 1933, Bonnie was the first to notice the posse and the crowd surrounding the camp. She cried out in alarm. Clyde fired his scattergun, and the officers returned fire. W.D. was struck in the chest by a ricochet bullet, Clyde was hit in the arm, and Bonnie was shot in the belly. Bonnie, Clyde, and W.D. waded across the Raccoon River that bordered the park. After stealing a car, they managed to escape.[60]

Their quick get-a-way was probably due to Buck and Blanche's predicament. Blanche had dragged Buck, who was trying to shoot the officers, into the underbrush, then behind a log. The law enforcement officers surrounded them and continued to shoot at Buck until Blanche screamed at them to stop, "You've already killed him!"[61]

Buck was taken to the local hospital, where he died five days later of pneumonia, with his mother by his side. Locked up in the county jail, Blanche never saw Buck again. Eventually, Blanche was convicted in Platte City, Missouri, for her role in the Red Crown Tourist Court shoot-out: ten years for harboring known criminals. She refused to speak about the gang and defiantly lied to the police to protect Clyde. But her outlaw days were over. She wrote many letters in prison, mostly to her father and to the Barrow family. After her release as an acknowledged model prisoner, she remarried a man who resembled Buck and became close friends with Bonnie's sister, Billie.[62]

On the Run

After the shoot-out, W.D. left the gang as soon as he could. He roamed the countryside as a migrant farm worker before being picked up and sent to prison, where he maintained that Clyde had kidnapped him, Bonnie was a willing accessory, and their life on the road was horrific. Despite his hand in killing several people, W.D. served only fifteen years, no doubt because of the confessions he readily made to Dallas police.[63]

Bonnie and Clyde now lived in a hell of their own making. They knew they couldn't stop anywhere for long out of fear of being caught. They essentially lived out of stolen cars. They slept along roadsides or parked in strangers' driveways with one eye always open.[64] They couldn't attend Buck's funeral in West Dallas. Clyde would drive hundreds of miles in one stretch, with Bonnie drinking, sleeping, or chatting in the passenger seat. The only distraction they had came from visits to illegal gambling parlors, where both were known to play a mean hand of cards.

A close-call with the law also made them very wary. During a family reunion with the Barrows and the Parkers, Dallas Sheriff Smoot Schmid and his posse laid an ambush, and several family members were caught in the volley of gunfire. Bonnie and Clyde made a successful get-a-way, but both had been shot in the knees. According to some accounts, Clyde was very angry over the unwarranted attack on his and Bonnie's family, and for a time staked out Smoot and Deputy Bob Alcorn's houses in Dallas to seek revenge.[65]

Slowly, Bonnie and Clyde nursed themselves back to health, but a kind of fatalism overtook their actions. Though Bonnie seemed to enjoy being half of a famous crime duo, Clyde became even more desperate. His next caper would be the crowning achievement of his life of crime: the raid on the Eastham Prison Farm.

The Eastham Raid

From Raymond's brother Floyd Hamilton, Clyde learned that former gang member Raymond Hamilton needed his help in staging a break-out at Eastham Prison Farm, where he had been sentenced to over 200 years in prison. James Mullins, a recently paroled convict whom Raymond Hamilton had promised $1,000 if he helped Floyd contact Clyde, served as the intermediary with knowledge of the work details on Eastham Farm.

Clyde was cool towards the plan at first. This may have been because, as author John Neal Phillips theorized, Raymond had left Clyde's fledgling gang in 1932 because he had wanted no part in an Eastham Raid. Clyde may have also not trusted the third man in the raid party, James Mullins, whose sole motive for the prison break was cash. However, Clyde understood that this could be a perfect opportunity to take revenge on Eastham and rebuild his gang. With Floyd Hamilton and James Mullins, Clyde and Bonnie drove to the prison farm north of Huntsville. On Sunday, Floyd visited Raymond and told him of the plan. That night, Floyd and James Mullins hid guns under a bridge in a culvert close to an area where the morning work detail would be. Fred Yost, a trusty from West Dallas, then took the guns and brought them to Raymond Hamilton and his friend, Joe Palmer.[66]

Raymond told several other inmates about the raid, most notably Henry Methvin, a man whom Clyde had befriended during his incarceration. Raymond also convinced Clyde to include Hilton Bybee in the escape plans, a convicted killer whom Raymond had befriended.[67] The escape was one big "friendly" reunion, no doubt!

The raid began in the early morning fog of January 16, 1934. Clyde, armed with either a machine gun or one of his "scatter gun" inventions, and James Mullins hid in the culvert to wait on the prison work detail. Bonnie waited in the car, composing a new poem. Her job was to sound the horn after she heard shots fired to help Clyde navigate his way back to the car in the heavy fog.

Raymond wasn't normally in the same work gang as Joe Palmer, Henry Methvin, and Hilton Bybee, but he accompanied them to their work site on this morning to be in closer proximity to the raid site. As the guards who patrolled the crew figured out what to do with Raymond, Joe Palmer quickly took out the gun hidden beneath his clothes, and Raymond Hamilton did the same. In the ensuing confusion, Palmer shot Major M.H. Crowson, who later died from his wounds.[68] Clyde shot over the heads of the guards. Raymond, Joe Palmer, Henry Methvin, Hilton Bybee, and an opportunist named Aubrey French then made their break. They followed the sound of Bonnie's honking and piled into the Ford V8. Driving at top speeds through various dusty and bumpy fields to avoid road blocks – with three men perched precariously in the rumble seat - Clyde let out Hilton Bybee and Aubrey French and then headed north.

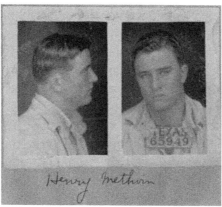

Henry Methvin had befriended Clyde at Eastham Prison Farm and became a constant partner after the Eastham Raid. In the movie *Bonnie and Clyde,* the character C.W. Moss is an amalgam of gang members W.D. Jones and Henry Methvin. Image courtesy of the Dallas Public Library.

Hilton Bybee was later caught in Amarillo. Joe Palmer, sick with TB, was let out in Wichita, Kansas, and then made his way to Joplin, Missouri, where he would receive periodic visits from Bonnie and Clyde. Some histories suggest that before Joe left for Joplin, he and Clyde killed Wade McNabb near Waskom, Texas. McNabb was a former accomplice who either owed them money or had threatened to turn them in.[69] In a confession to prison director Lee Simmons, Joe mentioned that Bonnie and Clyde would give him money when he needed it and Bonnie had once even bought him a suit.[70]

Raymond convinced Clyde to pick up Mary O'Dare in Wichita Falls, Texas. Mary, the wife of one of Raymond's many criminally-minded friends who was in prison at the time, dumped her lover-du-jour to ride with Raymond, Henry Methvin, Bonnie, and Clyde.

Mary O'Dare was not well liked by any in the gang, save for Raymond. Clyde called her a "washer-woman," and it was up to Bonnie to keep an eye on Mary lest she turn in the gang for reward money. Mary even suggested to Bonnie that she drug Clyde and take his money.[71]

At first, Clyde was elated to have his good friend Raymond Hamilton back in the gang, but his excitement quickly faded. Raymond, having been a minor celebrity in prison due to his association with Clyde Barrow, had become quite cocky. After a robbery of a bank in Lancaster, Texas, Clyde accused Raymond of pocketing more than his share of the money, and forced Raymond to leave the gang. Raymond and Mary then drove to Houston, and Bonnie, Clyde, and Henry Methvin continued on their own.[72]

Henry Methvin was a much larger man than Clyde but close to the same age. Like Clyde, he came from a poor family – his father was a some-time logger in rural Louisiana. He and Clyde became close friends, and Bonnie was like a sister to him. In the movie *Bonnie and Clyde*, the character C.W. Moss was a composite of W.D. Jones and Henry Methvin.

The poem that Bonnie had been composing while waiting in the car that cold January morning has become her most famous. She gave it to her mother on her last visit with her. The poem, *The Story of Bonnie and Clyde*, helped to ferment their legend.

You've read the story of Jesse James--
Of how he lived and died
If you're still in need
Of something to read
Here's the story of Bonnie and Clyde.

Now Bonnie and Clyde are the Barrow gang.
I'm sure you all have read
How they rob and steal
And those who squeal
Are usually found dying or dead.

There's lots of untruths to these write-ups
They're not so ruthless as that
Their nature is raw;
They hate the law--
The stool pigeons, spotters, and rats.

They call them cold-blooded killers
They say they are heartless and mean
But I say this with pride,
That I once knew Clyde
When he was honest and upright and clean.

But the laws fooled around,
Kept taking him down
And locking him up in a cell,
Till he said to me,
"I'll never be free,
So I'll meet a few of them in hell."

The road was so dimly lighted
There were no highway signs to guide
But they made up their minds

If all roads were blind,
They wouldn't give up till they died.

The road gets dimmer and dimmer
Sometimes you can hardly see
But it's fight, man to man,
And do all you can,
For they know they can never be free.

From heart-break some people have suffered
From weariness some people have died
But take it all in all,
Our troubles are small
Till we get like Bonnie and Clyde.

If a policeman is killed in Dallas,
And they have no clue or guide
If they can't find a fiend,
They just wipe their slate clean
And hang it on Bonnie and Clyde.

There's two crimes committed in America
Not accredited to the Barrow mob
They had no hand
In the kidnap demand,
Nor the Kansas City Depot job.

A newsboy once said to his buddy:
"I wish old Clyde would get jumped
In these awful hard times
We'd make a few dimes
If five or six cops would get bumped."

The police haven't got the report yet,
But Clyde called me up today,
He said, "Don't start any fights--
We aren't working nights--
We're joining the NRA."

From Irving to West Dallas viaduct
Is known as the Great Divide,
Where the women are kin,
And the men are men,
And they won't "stool" on Bonnie and Clyde.

If they try to act like citizens
And rent them a nice little flat,
About the third night
They're invited to fight
By a sub-gun's rat-tat-tat.

They don't think they're too smart or desperate,
They know that the law always wins
They've been shot at before,
But they do not ignore
That death is the wages of sin.

Some day they'll go down together
They'll bury them side by side
To few it'll be grief--
To the law a relief--
But it's death for Bonnie and Clyde.

Grapevine, Texas

On Easter Sunday, April 1, 1934, Bonnie, Clyde, and Henry waited to reunite with the Barrow and Parker families for a short visit. Bonnie had a bunny rabbit with her to give to her mother.[73] Law enforcement accounts maintained that Clyde had come to the area to meet with Raymond Hamilton, although at that time the police did not know that Raymond and Clyde were no longer working together. Clyde parked the stolen Ford on a small hill on Dove Road outside Grapevine, Texas. Two motorcycle officers, E.B. Wheeler and H.D. Murphy, noticed the car and wanted to see if the motorists were stranded. This was H.D. Murphy's first day on motorcycle patrol.

Upon hearing the motorcycles approach their car, Clyde told Henry, "Let's take them," meaning he had wanted to kidnap the officers. Instead, Henry mistook the meaning and opened fire, and then Clyde followed suit. Both officers were killed. The gang then sped away towards northeastern Oklahoma.[74]

The murder of the two highway patrol officers touched off a firestorm in Texas. According to newspapers and the public, the Barrow Gang had turned from romantic, desperate kids to hardened, sadistic criminals. Eyewitnesses appeared, claiming they saw a woman shoot one of the prone officers twice for good measure. The sheriff's office filmed a reenactment of the crime to show to movie audiences around the state. The police and the public both were desperate for some kind of justice, so Bonnie's sister Billie and Raymond's brother Floyd Hamilton were arrested for the murders. At the time of her arrest, Billie Parker Mace was dealing with the death of both of her children from an undiagnosed stomach ailment.[75]

The State Has Enough

Miriam "Ma" Ferguson, wife of the disgraced Governor Jim "Pa" Ferguson and the first female governor of Texas, had run her campaign on prison reform. She had already "cleaned house" in both the prison system and the Texas Rangers. With the public and law enforcement demanding Clyde Barrow's head on a platter, she took action.

Lee Simmons, the director of the Texas Prison System, had asked Governor Ferguson to issue a directive for hiring a Special Escape Investigator, whose sole mission would be to find the culprits responsible for the prison break at Eastham. After the Grapevine murders, she did just that. Though she was not a fan of ousted Texas Ranger Frank Hamer, she allowed Lee Simmons to hire him to organize an ambush.

Frank Hamer had been a Texas Ranger for decades prior to this special appointment. Well known and respected throughout the state and the law enforcement community, Hamer was tough, dependable, and singular in his pursuit for justice. Lee Simmons believed him to be the best man to take on (or take out) Clyde Barrow.

However, even a man of Hamer's stature (and swagger) could not tackle such an undertaking alone and soon a posse of well trained, level headed law men was formed who would hunt Clyde down with dogged determination.[76]

Well funded and with special jurisdiction to cover the entire state, the posse included Manny Gault of the Texas Highway Patrol and Dallas County Deputy Sheriffs Bob Alcorn and Ted Hinton.[77] Bob Alcorn was especially suited for the manhunt, as he knew Clyde by sight. Ted Hinton had grown up in West Dallas and was respected well enough by the Barrow family to pay visits to them, even though the family knew he was out to arrest their son.

Frank Hamer and Manny Gault partnered up, as did Ted Hinton and Bob Alcorn. These men remained partners on this case until a warm, sunny May morning in 1934. The hunt for Clyde took them through several states and along dirt roads. Towards the end, they lived like Clyde and Bonnie did: in their cars, always on the look-out, and always, always driving.

Route 66 Murder

Meanwhile, Bonnie, Clyde, and Henry had fled to Ottowa County in northeastern Oklahoma to hide out after the Grapevine murders. This mining area, a hodge-podge of jurisdictional boundaries encompassing the Cherokee, Peoria, Quapaw, Modoc, Ottawa, Shawnee, Wyandotte, and Senenca nations, had always seemed appealing to Clyde – the region, with its gambling halls and hard-living mining folk, was known as a good place for outlaws to get lost.

As the gang parked on a country road off Route 66 to catch up on sleep, City Marshall Percy Boyd and Constable Cal Campbell from Commerce, Oklahoma approached the car to check up on them. As was usual for the jumpy gang, panic ensued. Clyde shot and wounded Percy Boyd, and Henry shot and killed Cal Campbell.

The Ambush Posse consisted of (from back to front, left to right): Ted Hinton of the Dallas County Sheriff's Department, Prentice Oakeley of the Bienville Parish Sheriff's Department, Manny Gault of the Texas Highway Patrol, Bob Alcorn of the Dallas County Sheriff's Department, Henderson Jordon of the Bienville Parish Sheriff's Department, and Frank Hamer of the Texas Rangers. Image courtesy of the Dallas Public Library.

In their attempt to flee, Clyde got the car stuck in a ditch. Several passers-by (farmers, other motorists) stood by to watch him, while others offered assistance to the downed man. Clyde waved his gun around and commandeered some of the bystanders to help him get his car out. The scene must have played out like a bad sit-com. The locals, entranced by this slow-moving get-a-way, watched with morbid fascination as Clyde frantically pulled his car out of the ditch, cursing to himself and threatening everyone within ear shot. When the gang finally got moving, Clyde had to dodge parked cars and weave around the spectators in what must have been the oddest moment of his life.[78]

To ensure their getaway, the gang took Percy Boyd hostage. As they drove around at high speeds, Bonnie talked for a while with Boyd, telling him that despite the infamous photo of her, she didn't really smoke cigars. He also listened to the gang's grandstanding; though Clyde told him he was sorry that Cal

Campbell had been killed, all three acted very cocky about their crimes. Percy Boyd, who upon his release after a day's worth of driving was immediately interviewed, recalled that the gang seemed to have no concept of what they were doing – their whole crime spree was like one big game to them, and they believed themselves too smart for the law. Boyd also mistook Henry Methvin for Raymond Hamilton, as neither he nor anyone else knew of the rift between Raymond and Clyde at that time.[79]

Clyde, Henry, and Bonnie drove on to Joplin, Missouri to pick up Joe Palmer, who helped them rob a bank in Iowa. Joe then returned to Joplin, was arrested, and was sent back to Texas to stand trial for Major Crowson's murder. As the gang drove through Topeka, Kansas, Clyde stole a Ford Fordor Deluxe Sedan, newly purchased by Ruth Warren, right out of her driveway.[80]

Clyde then made a fateful decision: for a while, he, Bonnie, and Henry would hide out near Henry Methvin's family in northern Louisiana.

No One's Loving Raymond

The gang headed to Louisiana. Ten miles south of Gibsland, a small town on US 80 that sits in the middle of a dense forest, Clyde either purchased, rented, or squatted in an abandoned dogtrot house that was owned by Otis Cole. When he went somewhere, Clyde would pose as a lumberjack.

During this time, Raymond Hamilton's luck began to run out. He parted ways with Mary O'Dare, who not only spilled the beans to the police about Raymond's antics, but also added important information about the current members of the Barrow Gang.[81] When Raymond and a drifter friend robbed a bank in Lewisville, Texas, in April 1934, authorities quickly apprehended him in Howe, then sent him to Denton County. He made the rounds, standing trial in the various counties where he was wanted.

After his capture, Clyde sent Raymond a note in which he called him "yellow" and taunted him to try to talk his way out of the electric chair.[82] Clyde's "advice" notwithstanding, Raymond was given the death penalty for his role in the murders of John

Bucher of Hillsboro and Major Crowson of Eastham Prison. Raymond gained even more notoriety for staging a daring escape from the Huntsville Prison's death house in 1935 with his old accomplice, Joe Palmer. However, Raymond and Joe were caught. They were quickly executed, Raymond following just a few hours after Joe's own date with destiny.

Louisiana Hide-Out

The spring of 1934 proved hot and muggy, especially in Louisiana. Life on the lam was starting to take its toll on Bonnie and Clyde. Both had seemed to age considerably - Bonnie began wearing her hair in a bobbed perm and walked with considerable effort, and Clyde had grown a mustache - and both looked wearily at the camera during a May 6th meeting with extended family members along a logging road in East Texas. This would be their last family reunion.

They did get help from Henry Methvin's family, a poor but tight-knit clan of Louisiana loggers. Suspicious of the laws, they had been supplying Bonnie and Clyde with food and other basic comforts so that the duo could stay out of the public's eye as much as possible. Word still got out that a strange couple had set up residence in a dilapidated dogtrot not far from the little hamlet of Lebanon.[83]

With the arrest of Raymond Hamilton, Frank Hamer learned that the man with Bonnie and Clyde was Henry Methvin, one of the escapees from the Eastham Prison Raid. The entire tracking posse hurried to Louisiana. They hoped that the Methvin family would cooperate with their investigation to help them find Clyde. Or, if they were really, really lucky, maybe Clyde was hiding out in Louisiana, and they could catch him there.

On May 19, 1934, Bonnie, Clyde, and Henry visited downtown Shreveport. They may have been casing a place to rob or were just hanging out to get away from the backwoods heat. Bonnie and Clyde sat in the car as Henry went to wash clothes in a laundromat and pick up sandwiches at a diner. When a police car surprised them, Clyde drove off in an hurry, leaving Henry behind. Shreveport police gave chase but aborted it quickly.

However, the police were pretty sure it was Clyde driving the car. Henry was not arrested.[84]

Apparently, the trio had decided that if they were ever separated, they would rendezvous back at Henry's parents' house, and on the morning of May 23, 1934, that's what Bonnie and Clyde decided to do.

Buggy Morning

Much has been written about the deadly ambush on Bonnie and Clyde. Modern accounts agree that the Methvins had come to a bargain with the ambush posse as led by Frank Hamer: if they helped to set up Bonnie and Clyde, Henry would receive leniency from the State of Texas. This plot was revealed in Henry's own testimony while on trial for the murder of Cal Campbell in Miami, Oklahoma.[85]

However, the accounts from the men who took part in the ambush offer considerably different versions as to Henry Methvin's complicity. Although Henry's role in the deaths of Bonnie and Clyde was revealed as early as 1936, Frank Hamer's biographers (1968) and Ted Hinton's memoirs (1979) maintained that no overt deals with the Methvins were made.

According to *I'm Frank Hamer: The Life of a Texas Peace Officer*, Frank Hamer had kept surveillance around Bienville Parish for quite some time and knew intimate details about the criminals' routines and habits – much of this information, he related, was obtained from friends and family of the Methvins. Armed with this knowledge, Frank Hamer planned an ambush next to a stump where newspapers, letters, notes, and other "mail" were hidden for Clyde to read. Knowing that Clyde would visit the hiding place at some point soon, he and the other officers camped out across from the stump. Here, the officers would give Bonnie and Clyde an opportunity to surrender – or for the officers to shoot.[86]

In his book *Ambush*, Ted Hinton described how he and fellow Dallas Sheriff's Deputy Bob Alcorn had been casing the thickets around the Methvin home for days. From the Shreveport Police, they had learned of the encounter with Clyde and Henry on May 19, and they believed their chance to get Clyde may have finally arrived. Together with Frank Hamer, Manny Gault, Sheriff Henderson Jordon, and Deputy Prentiss Oakley, the latter two from Bienville Parish, they staked out the narrow road that led to the Methvin farm to stage an ambush from the side of the road.

Ted Hinton insisted that the posse had not made any deals with the Methvins. Instead, armed with the scant information that they may run into Clyde along the road to the Methvin house, they just chanced an encounter with Ivy Methvin's truck early in the morning of May 23. Because they supposed that Ivy Methvin hadn't gone for an early morning ride but had probably been out looking for Clyde, the posse stopped him and handcuffed him to a tree. The officers then decided to use Ivy Methvin's truck as a decoy in case Clyde should drive down the road. They took off a tire and parked the truck facing north east.

Lee Simmons, Head of the Texas Prison System, wrote in his memoir, *Assignment Huntsville: Memoirs of a Texas Prison Official* (1957) that Henry Methvin's father Ivy had approached Frank Hamer. Frank Hamer promised to show Henry leniency in sentencing if Ivy cooperated with the investigation. Ivy agreed, either with or without Henry's knowledge. On a rendezvous date set up by Henry and Clyde, Ivy would pretend his truck had broken down, which would force Clyde to stop long enough for a clear shot. This all would take place around May 23. [87]

Swollen from mosquito bites, tired, dirty, and cranky, the posse, hiding in the underbrush, felt that whether they got Clyde now or not, they were going to go home. They missed their families and decent meals. Then, on that warm, humid morning of May 23, they heard the familiar whirr of a powerful Ford V8, coming fast from the northwest.

End of the Road

The road from Mount Lebanon was typical for rural Louisiana. It was graveled, narrow, and surrounded by thick underbrush and large pine trees. Ivy Methvin's truck sat on a straight-a-way, and was quite visible to Clyde as he crested the incline. Because Clyde recognized the Methvin's Ford Model A, he slowed down.

Bonnie and Clyde had ordered breakfast earlier at Canfield's Café in Gibsland. As they drove southwest to Methvin's house, Bonnie was eating her sandwich and studying a map. She was looking rather smart in a sequined tam hat and with an acorn broach pinned to the lapel of her red dress. Clyde was driving in stocking feet – he liked to drive without shoes – with a shotgun wedged between his legs and the car door.[88] He was wearing shades to guard against the sun's glare.[89] A logging truck was approaching in the distance. The time was a little after nine in the morning.

As Clyde slowly passed Methvin's truck, either Frank Hamer yelled or Bob Alcorn shouted, "Halt!" However, Bienville Sheriff Henderson Jordan and Deputy Prentiss Oakley later recalled

Louisiana Highway 154 today, looking towards the northeast. Clyde would have crested the hill and seen Ivy Methvin's truck at the bottom. Photo by author.

that no one had asked Bonnie and Clyde to surrender.[90]

The posse started shooting. The volley of bullets rocked the car so ferociously that the men thought Clyde was trying to speed away.[91] Clyde was killed instantly, but Bonnie screamed as it dawned on her what was happening.

While the hail of bullets lasted only a few seconds, they landed squarely on its targets. Clyde was shot through the head, neck, shoulders, and even the legs. Bonnie was riddled through the side; her face became distorted by a rifle shot, which shattered her teeth. Even the fingers of her right hand, which she probably had held up in her last living act, had been blown off.

Along a nondescript road in the thickets of northern Louisiana, just south of Highway 80, the highway which they had driven so many times throughout their short lives, this young, brazen couple died as they had lived: in a car, on the run, and together.

Spectacle in Louisiana

The lawmen inspected the car after the ambush. They found that during the volley, the car, still in gear, had lurched forward to end up with the drivers' side wedged against an embankment. Ted Hinton opened the passenger door and caught Bonnie as she spilled out. He gently placed her back into her seat, this time leaning her against Clyde.[92] He then recorded the death scene with a 16 mm camera to use for the death inquiry and investigation that would follow. This film soon made it to the newsreels, and movie theaters remained packed for months – everyone wanted to glimpse the demise of the most notorious gangster duo in recent American history.

Upon inspection, the posse found several automatic rifles, license plates, camping gear, food, clothes, and a saxophone in the back of the car. They called for the coroner, and the next task they assumed was to protect the car from the many curious who had heard the gunfire and wanted to investigate. As word got around that the infamous duo Bonnie and Clyde had been shot on the Mount Lebanon to Ringgold Road, it seemed like everyone came out of the woodwork to watch the macabre scene. Some misguided souls even tried to saw off Clyde's trigger finger and ears.[93]

The car, with Bonnie and Clyde still inside, was towed all the way to Arcadia, where the Conger Furniture Store doubled as a funeral parlor. As luck would have it, the wrecker broke down in front of the school in Gibsland, and children spilled out to view the carnage for themselves. One little girl fainted from the sight of Bonnie's ruined face.[94]

Once in Arcadia, the crowd grew bigger. People pushed and shoved their way through the throngs to witness this spectacle first hand. As the bodies were placed onto boards and moved into the store, ladies dipped their handkerchiefs in the blood that was still flowing out of the wounds; others chipped so much glass from the "death car" that the entire rear driver's side window went missing.[95]

The kids at the Gibsland School received a graphic lesson that crime doesn't pay. Photo by author.

Frank Hamer first contacted prison director Lee Simmons of the successful ambush, who then notified the Texas governor. Reporters from Arcadia and Shreveport quickly relayed the information to their Dallas brethren. One reporter called Emma Parker, who fainted when she heard the news.[96]

Henry Barrow was taken to Arcadia to accompany his son back home. People there remembered him as an old and frail man whose quiet weeping silenced many who believed this gruesome carnival to be the best show in town.

Legends

Bonnie, who had asked her mother to "take her home" when she died, could not be laid out in her mother's living room after all. Once in Dallas, the curious came in droves to see the bodies lying in their open caskets, and their number was far too large for the families to handle. People stood in line for hours to

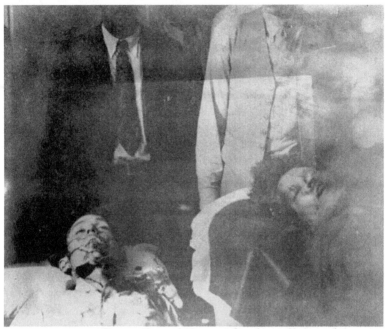

A gruesome scene at Conger Funeral Home. After the staff cleaned them up, the coroner examined the bodies. Image courtesy of the Dallas Public Library.

catch a glimpse of the bodies. While those who visited Bonnie, who could be viewed at a funeral home along upscale Forest Avenue, did so respectfully, a circus atmosphere surrounded Clyde's funeral, whose remains were on view in the Victorian neighborhood along Ross Avenue. [97]

For the public, the funerals provided cruel entertainment. Clyde's family was taunted by crowds of rowdy young men. Newspaper boys apparently donated a large wreath to Clyde in gratitude of the many newspapers his antics helped to sell.

Photographers snapped away even in the most private moments of grief.[98] Bonnie's sister Billie felt so overwhelmed she had to leave. The Parkers had been especially hard hit – not only was Bonnie dead, but Billie had lost both of her children fairly recently. She herself had been incarcerated because she was under suspicion for the Grapevine murders.[99]

Clyde's funeral in May, 1934, was *the* biggest event in Dallas. Image courtesy of the Dallas Public Library.

Yet another wish of Bonnie's would not be granted – she and Clyde were not buried together. Emma Parker had considered Clyde almost abusive in the way he was able to influence Bonnie, and she refused this request.[100] Instead, Clyde shared a tombstone with his brother Buck at Western Heights Cemetery in Oak Cliff. Bonnie was at first interred at Fish Trap Cemetery in West Dallas, but was later moved to Crown Hill Memorial Park just northwest of downtown, where she was put to rest with her deceased niece and nephew. Years later, her mother was buried in the same plot.

In 1935, family members and associates had to stand trial for harboring Clyde Barrow, a wanted fugitive, and the trial became one of the more sensational ones in Dallas County's history. Bonnie's sister Billie Parker Mace received a year in jail, and their mothers, Emma Parker and Cumie Barrow, both had to serve thirty days. The male gang members received up to two years for their roles in refusing to tell the law Clyde's whereabouts.

As the female defendants are led into the courthouse at the Bonnie and Clyde harboring trial, Billie Parker Mace looks directly into the camera. Image courtesy of the Dallas Public Library.

Within a few years, the furor over Bonnie and Clyde had died down. Gradually, only their families remembered things as they were, and the story of Bonnie and Clyde turned into a Texas tale. Their lives and times, shrouded in a mist of nostalgia, sensationalism, and exaggeration, became fodder for a legend that has been passed down in the state from generation to generation. That legend, encased forever in a 1967 movie that proved to be one of cinema's greatest accomplishments, is as strong today as ever.

And through the haziness of legends, myths, and truths, we drive down the lonely roads, visit the forgotten buildings, and capture the haunting landscapes that retrace the steps of these infamous, outlaw lovers.

Whatever Happened To...?

The "Death Car"

Ruth Warren retrieved her stolen – and now ruined - Ford Fordor Sedan from Louisiana, but first she had to take the sheriff to court, who demanded $15,000 for it. No doubt sitting on a towel and with the windows rolled down, she drove it and its gore to Shreveport. She then had it towed back to Topeka. Throughout the years, Ruth Warren rented the car to various carnival sideshows. Eventually, a man in Florida who owned a museum of the "macabre and infamous" bought the car, and after he died, the Primm Valley Resort (Nevada) acquired it. Along with Clyde's bullet riddled shirt, it is now on display behind glass at the Primm Valley Resort Casino.

The Contents of the "Death Car"

Lee Simmons told Frank Hamer that he and the other men in the ambush could pick out any items out of the car to have as "souvenirs." Many of the guns taken from the Death Car are now on display at the Texas Rangers Museum in Waco, Texas. Other items, such as Bonnie's acorn brooch, were taken by a number of people, and from time to time these authentic Bonnie and Clyde paraphernalia surface in the collector's world. The Barrows and the Parkers both asked for the items in the car, as they maintained that the lack of a search warrant precluded any confiscation. Instead, the only things the families were able to retrieve were the clothes that the couple had been wearing.

Eastham Prison Farm and the Walls Unit

The Eastham Prison Farm is still within the Texas Department of Corrections, though the original building is now only a shell. A newer unit has been erected on the original grounds. The fortress-like Walls Unit still dominates downtown Huntsville. The interesting Texas Prison Museum in Huntsville displays "Old Sparky," the very electric chair on which Raymond Hamilton and Joe Palmer received their penance.

W.D. Jones

After being caught in Texas, W.D. Jones gave a lengthy deposition on his dealings with Clyde Barrow. He claimed that the gang had held him against his will, though he had been more than willing to shoot his share of victims. He served a fifteen year sentence and afterwards, moved to Houston, where he worked in various low wage jobs and took up a drug habit. Upon the release of the movie *Bonnie and Clyde*, he gave an informative interview with Playboy Magazine. Murdered in 1974, he is buried in Houston.

Blanche Barrow

While serving a ten year sentence (reduced to five years) as an exemplary inmate in a Missouri prison, Blanche renewed correspondence with her father, and also tried to stay in touch with the Barrows. After she was paroled, she moved back to Dallas, where she found work as a waitress. Eventually, she remarried and formed a close friendship with Bonnie's sister Billie. She also penned an insightful memoir, which was edited and released by John Neal Phillips in 2004 after her death in 1988. She is buried under her married name Frasure in Dallas, next to her third husband.

Cumie and Henry Barrow

Both Cumie and Henry had to stand trial for harboring their fugitive son in Dallas, and both received mild sentences. Living in the midst of West Dallas, where old associates and young punks harassed them, Clyde's parents knew little peace even after his death. Their station was firebombed, and in a drive-by shooting, Cumie lost one of her eyes. Hardship defined their lives. Both are buried next to Clyde and Buck's grave in Western Heights Cemetery.

Emma Parker

Like Cumie Barrow, Emma had to serve thirty days in jail for harboring fugitives. Emma remained in Dallas, where she lived at various addresses. After a battle with cancer, she was buried in Bonnie's plot at the Crown Hill Cemetery in Northwest Dallas.

Billie Parker Mace

Billie was sentenced to a year in prison for harboring and aiding the fugitives. Still reeling from losing her children and sister, Billie recovered slowly, but never had more children. She lived quietly in Dallas, though she did grant interviews about her sister. She is buried in Dallas.

Roy Thornton

Bonnie's husband spent the rest of his life in and out of jail. He was killed in 1937 when he tried to escape Eastham State Prison Farm.

Henry Methvin

Despite the plea bargain with the State of Texas that he made for his role in the ambush, Henry still served ten years in an Oklahoma prison for the murder of Cal Campbell (although he was originally given the death penalty). He moved back to Louisiana and worked as a bar tender. He died after being run over by a train in 1948.

Ted Hinton

After the ambush, Ted Hinton spent more years in law enforcement, culminating in the position of a Deputy U.S. Marshall. After his service in World War II, he owned a motor lodge. His film, taken in the aftermath of the shooting, became world famous, and he authored an interesting and detailed account on his role in tracking down the gang, *Ambush*. He died in 1977 and is buried in Dallas. His son, Boots Hinton, co-owns the Bonnie and Clyde Museum in Gibsland, Louisiana.

Frank Hamer

A lifelong Texas Ranger, Frank Hamer received a special congressional citation for his role in tracking Bonnie and Clyde. After the ambush, he became a special agent for the Texas Rangers, being recalled on occasion to bust strikes, maintain order in dangerous situations, and supervise contested elections. He died in his sleep in 1955 and is buried in Austin. His life was recounted by H. Gordon Frost and John Holmes Jenkins in a 1968 book, *I'm Frank Hamer.*

The Victims

No one who goes on a journey to discover the history of Bonnie and Clyde should forget that the victims of their crimes were not just those who died. The families they left behind told of economic and psychological hardships, as their main breadwinners and heads of household were killed during one of America's worst depressions. Without their fathers, children had to leave school to earn money to keep the family farms afloat. Women who were widowed with young children had to seek work wherever they could find it. These murders occurred in the era before Social Security (though FDR implemented the system by the late 1930s), and many of the victims' families became destitute. The Barrow Gang wrecked more havoc than they could have ever imagined.

Traveling History

Evidence of the past in Joplin, Missouri. Photo by author.

Discovering Depression-era sights in the Southwest and Midwest is exciting enough. Coupled with a notorious history, traveling can be even more rewarding. With an itinerary in one hand, this book in another, and an active imagination, you can put a "place" behind all the scenes that you've read about.

Photos only do a small amount of justice – understanding and reliving history by exploration is not only more informative, but also a lot more fun.

The Traveling History of Bonnie and Clyde will take you all over middle America. These trips can be taken in short spurts, or in one long road trip that may take three days or more. You'll be meandering along stretches of roads that Clyde Barrow raced down, driving through towns that witnessed the hardships of the Depression, and winding your way through lesser-known streets of Dallas.

The sites are listed along with touring information, with occasional detours and "Blasts from the Past." Meant to be an "active history" of landmarks, all directions originate from Dallas. Also, make sure to bring a detailed map as you travel to these places!

Tour 1 – The Stomping Ground Trip

Dallas, Texas (1 leisurely day, though "leisurely" depends on what you want to see and skip).

For those of you who just want to get your toes wet, this short, one day tour will get you started on the immediate history of Bonnie and Clyde. You will be spending some time in West Dallas – newspaper reporters in the 1930s called this area a "Little Cicero" and, while the shot-gun houses are mostly gone, West Dallas is still a little on the dilapidated side. This tour will also bring you into the "tourist Mecca" of Dallas: the old courthouse, Dealy Plaza, and the world-famous Texas School Book Depository.

But beware – Dallas is re-inventing itself once again, and one of the targeted redevelopment areas is West Dallas, where the first few sites of the tour are located. So go out there and see these places before development takes over!

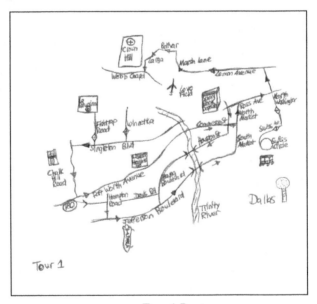

Tour 1 Routes

West Dallas - Barrow Star Service Station - La Reunion Cemetery - Cement City Elementary School - Western Heights Cemetery - Oak Cliff and Viaducts – Downtown Dallas (Dallas County Criminal Courts, Old Red Courthouse, Dealy Plaza, Triple Underpass, and Sixth Floor Museum)- Dallas Bar Association (Sparkman Holtz Funeral Home) – Swiss Avenue Circle Street Car Stop - Crown Hill Memorial Park

West Dallas
4000-3000 blocks of North Winnetka Avenue
Dallas, Texas
Directions:
1) Interstate 35 East
2) Sylvan Avenue exit west (cross Trinity River)
3) Right onto Singleton Boulevard
4) Right onto North Winnetka Avenue.
-Or-
1) Downtown Dallas
2) Commerce Street Bridge west over the Trinity River
3) Follow Commerce Street until it turns into Singleton Boulevard, then follow Singleton.
4) Turn right onto North Winnetka Avenue.
What's to See:
    Many of Clyde's associates lived around this road, chief among them the Hamilton family. Raymond's mother's house sits at the left (west) corner of Singleton Boulevard and Winnetka Avenue. At the 3100 block of Winnetka Avenue is the home once occupied by Lillian McBride, sister to gang member Raymond Hamilton (in 1932, the address was 507 County Avenue). Clyde shot and killed Dallas County Deputy Sheriff Malcolm Davis on the fort porch. The house still looks like it did in the 1930s, but because it's a private residence, please DO NOT disturb anyone.

The gas station in 2004, where Henry Barrow once sold Texaco gas and cold drinks. Photo by author.

Barrow "Star" Service Station
1221 Singelton Boulevard
Dallas, Texas
Directions:
1) From North Winnetka Drive, go south back to Singleton Boulevard.
2) Turn right (west) onto Singleton Boulevard. The station is a block to your right.
What's to See:

Henry Barrow sold Texaco gas from two pumps, as well as cold drinks and snacks. The Barrow family lived in two rooms attached to the gas station. From where Henry Barrow pumped gas, he commanded a great view of the Dallas skyline. The service station was built from wood, but throughout the years it has been bricked, painted, then painted again, so there's not much of the original building left. The neighborhood surrounding the station is still quite "seedy," which puts the service station in an "authentic" context.

La Reunion Cemetery
Fish Trap Road (no address)
Singleton Boulevard
Dallas, Texas

Directions:
1) From the Star Service Station, go west on Singleton Boulevard (away from downtown Dallas)
2) Turn right (north) onto Fish Trap Road. Follow the road past the Fish Trap lake.
3) At the northern end of the lake, take an unnamed street to the left. On the right (north) side is a chain link fence that surrounds the now disused cemetery.

What's to See:
Bonnie was first buried at La Reunion Cemetery, though her grave was moved to Crown Hill Memorial Park close to Love Field in the 1940s. Her grandparents, the Krauses, remain buried here. La Reunion Cemetery is also the last home of many "La Reunion" settlers. La Reunion was an experiment by Swiss, French, and Belgian immigrants who, in the 1850s, wanted to create a socialist community around the Trinity River. That didn't work, and their descendents went on to become the workers and civic leaders of burgeoning Dallas.

Bonnie's Grade School in Cement City
1601 Chalk Hill Road
Dallas, Texas
Directions:
1) From La Reunion Cemetery, return south to Singleton Boulevard.
2) At Singleton Boulevard, turn right (west).
3) Turn left (south) onto Chalk Hill Road.
4) Travel south on Chalk Hill Road approximately 4 miles. You will pass under the Interstate 30 bridge (no access to Interstate).
5) The school will be on your right after the underpass.

Bonnie shined as a student at the Cement City grade school, which now houses a security company. Photo by author.

What's to See:

   The old brick school building, garishly painted, is now home to a private business. A chain link fence, and the dogs behind it, guard the school from vandals, who have used the school for target practice over the years. Told you it's not the best neighborhood!

Clyde, Buck and other Barrow Graves
Western Heights Cemetery, Fort Worth Avenue (no address)
Dallas, Texas
Directions
1) From the school, take Chalk Hill Road south until it intersects with TX 180/ Davis Road.
2) Turn left (east) onto Davis Road.
3) Follow Davis Road to the east until the split with Fort Worth Avenue. Stay left to continue east on Fort Worth Avenue.
4) You will travel about 4 miles and will cross over Interstate 30.
5) Western Heights Cemetery will be on your left between Navarro and Neal Streets.
What's to See:

   A small cemetery with many immigrant graves, the Barrows (Clyde and Buck share a tomb stone) are buried along a fence row on the west side. A chain link fence and locked gate discourages vandals. In the past, some misguided souls have actually stolen Clyde's tomb stone, including a city councilman from Oklahoma City, who, during a visit to Dallas for the University of Texas/ University of Oklahoma football game, stole the stone and used it back home as a coffee table. You can be an upstanding citizen and call (214) 224-8222 to obtain access, or just find a hole in the fence. You did not read that here.

The Texas Theater greets the passer-by in downtown Oak Cliff. Photo by author.

Blasts from the Past: Oak Cliff's "Spine" and the Viaducts
Directions:
1) From Western Heights Cemetery, turn right (west) onto Fort Forth Avenue. You will drive over Interstate 30 once again.
2) Turn left (south) onto Hampton Road and follow it to TX 180/ Davis Road.
3) Turn left (east) onto Davis Road to drive towards downtown Dallas.
4) Turn right (south) onto TX 354/ Zang Boulevard.
5) At the intersection of Zang Boulevard and Jefferson Boulevard, turn left (east) onto East Jefferson Boulevard.
         -or-
1) From Western Heights Cemetery, turn right (west) onto Fort Worth Avenue. You will drive over Interstate 30 once again.
2) Turn left (south) onto Hampton Road.

3) Turn left (east) onto West Jefferson Boulevard (you will drive through the intersection of Hampton Road and TX 180/ Davis Road). West Jefferson Boulevard becomes East Jefferson Boulevard past the intersection with Zang Boulevard.

What's to See

As you drive along this urban landscape, you'll be in the midst of vintage Dallas, with brick-faced store fronts from the 1920s to the 1940s gracing the many areas of Oak Cliff, the oldest city in Dallas. You will also pass by the Texas Theater where Lee Harvey Oswald was apprehended after shooting both President John F. Kennedy and Police Officer J.D. Tippit.

As you continue heading east on Jefferson Boulevard, notice the old diners, neon, and the chalky cliffs from which Oak Cliff gets its name. You will drive to downtown Dallas over the Trinity River on the Jefferson Boulevard Viaduct. While on the bridge, make sure to notice the concrete bridge that will be to your north (left). That is the Houston Street Viaduct, the first permanent bridge built over the Trinity after the 1908 Trinity River flood and the longest concrete bridge in the world. Clyde Barrow's family camped out under this bridge before moving to West Dallas. He also met future gang member W.D. Jones underneath the piers.

Downtown Dallas
- Dealy Plaza (Houston, Commerce, and Main Streets)
- Dallas County Criminal Courts Building (100 South Houston Street)
- Old Red Courthouse Museum (100 South Houston Street)
- Sixth Floor Museum (411 Elm Street)
- Triple Underpass (Elm, Commerce, and Main Streets)
Dallas, Texas
Directions:
1) After crossing the Jefferson viaduct, Jefferson Boulevard becomes South Market Street (FM 354).
2) Follow South Market Street and take a left (south) onto Elm Street.
3) Dealy Plaza, the Dallas County Criminal Courts Building, the Old Red Courthouse Museum, the Sixth Floor Museum, and the

Triple Underpass are located at the intersections of Elm Street and Houston Street.

4) You can park at the Sixth Floor Museum (follow signs) or in a parking garage under the courthouse by turning left onto Houston Street and once again turning left onto Commerce Street. Notice that no parking is free over here!

The restored Dallas County Courthouse, nicknamed "Old Red," now houses a museum. Photo by author.

What's to See:

The Dallas County Criminal Courts Building used to house the jail from which Raymond Hamilton escaped during his brief tenure in crime. A red bricked, federal style building with many art deco touches, the courts building also witnessed Jack Ruby's trial. Next door is the Old Red Courthouse, a Romanesque structure from Texas' "Golden Age" of Courthouse construction, complete with gargoyles. Inside is an extensive museum chronicling the history of Dallas County. Along with all other Dallasites, the Barrows and the Parkers conducted their business here. Marco's Café, where Bonnie once served Ted

Hinton, used to be on southern Houston Street, but other buildings have taken its place.

Dealy Plaza (named after the publisher of the Dallas Morning News), the infamous Triple Underpass, and the Sixth Floor Museum, from where Lee Harvey Oswald changed history with a single (or more) shot(s), are worth a stop as well. The orange building that houses the Sixth Floor Museum is the old Dallas School Book Depository. Built in the early 20th century, it was used as a warehouse for storing farm implements in the 1930s.

Dealy Plaza is the original founding site of Dallas. Just to throw a little more trivia into all this heavy history: the area where the Sixth Floor Museum is located was once called "Frogtown," home to brothels, cribs, and gambling halls prior to the Civil War.

Dallas Bar Association
Formerly Sparkman-Holtz Funeral Home, site of Clyde's funeral
2101 Ross Avenue
Dallas, Texas
Directions:
1) From Dealy Plaza, take Houston Street to the south – it's a one-way street, so it's the only way you can go.
2) Turn left onto Commerce Street. Note: If you parked in the underground garage by the Old Red Courthouse, you must turn left onto Commerce Street.
3) Turn left onto North Market Street
4) Turn right onto Ross Avenue.
5) The old funeral home, where Clyde's send-off brought thousands of curious on-lookers and today houses the Dallas Bar Association, will be at the corner of Ross Avenue and Olive Street.
What's to See:
Inside the last of many grand Victorian residences that used to grace Ross Avenue, the Dallas Bar Association displays photographs of the circus-like atmosphere that was Clyde Barrow's funeral. Call 214-220-7400 to schedule a visit. Close

by are also the renowned Dallas Museum of Art and the Nasher Sculpture Center.

Bonnie used to work here – today, Clyde's Body Shop occupies the space. Photo by author.

Swiss Circle Street Car Stop
Site of Hargrave's Café, where Bonnie was a waitress
3308 Swiss Circle
Dallas, Texas
Directions:
1) From the Dallas Bar Association house, take Ross Avenue left (northeast).
2) Just before the Interstate 45 Overpass, Ross Avenue jogs to the southwest as it briefly becomes a one-way street in the opposite direction. Follow Boll Street to the right for a hundred feet, then turn left onto San Jacinto Street. After you make this small detour, you will meet up again with Ross Avenue.
3) Turn right (south) onto North Washington.
4) Turn right (southwest) onto Swiss Avenue.
5) Continue on Swiss Avenue to Swiss Circle on your left (south).
6) Hargraves Café was situated amidst the semi-circular, low-slung, strip-mall buildings which are today nestled against a Baylor Hospital parking garage.

What's to See:

In the 1920s, Bonnie worked as a waitress at Hargrave's Café at the Swiss Circle street car stop. Bonnie took the street car back and forth from home to work.

Bonnie's, Emma's and Billie's Children's Graves

Crown Hill Memorial Park
9700 Webb Chapel Road
Dallas, Texas

Directions:

1) From Swiss Circle, back-track northeast to North Washington Street.
2) Turn left (north) onto North Washington Street until it intersects with Lemon Avenue.
3) Turn left (northwest) onto Lemon Avenue.
4) Follow Lemon Avenue northwest for approximately 5 miles. (You will pass Love Field Airport and the Frontiers of Flight Museum, a museum well worth your visit.)
5) Just north of Love Field Airport, Lemon Avenue turns into Marsh Lane. Continue north on Marsh Lane.
6) Turn left (west) onto Bolivar Drive until Bolivar Drive ends at Larga Drive next to Crown Hill Memorial Park.
7) Turn left (south) onto Larga Drive.
8) Immediately turn right (west) onto Webb Chapel Road.
9) The entrance to Crown Hill Memorial Park will be on your right.

What's to See:

Bonnie Parker is buried in the center of Crown Hill Memorial Park. Near her grave also rest her niece and nephew, both of whom died of some kind of stomach ailment within days of each other (may have been polio), and her mother, Emma Parker.

To find Bonnie's grave, park on the left (west) side of the Mausoleum. Follow the tall hedgerow on the west side to approximately the middle. Bonnie's grave will be nestled against the hedgerow near cedar trees on the western side of the hedges. Her epitaph reads:

AS THE FLOWERS ARE ALL MADE SWEETER BY
THE SUNSHINE AND THE DEW,
SO THIS OLD WORLD IS MADE BRIGHTER BY
THE LIVES OF FOLKS LIKE YOU.

Near Bonnie's grave lie her niece, nephew and her mother, Emma. Photo by author.

Tour 2 – The Historical Trip

Dallas, Tarrant, Kaufman, Collin, and Denton Counties (1 long day, or a day and a half).

A tour of the places that surround the city of Dallas offers a glimpse into the lives of not only Bonnie and Clyde, but also of the regular people who lived in the 1930s. The cities and counties on this tour comprise the Dallas/Fort Worth Metroplex. This is a great scenic road trip, especially as you follow so many old roads. Belt Line Road, the original loop around Dallas County, and TX 180 (the former US 80, or "Bankhead Highway") are especially "vintage."
Note that all directions originate from Dallas.

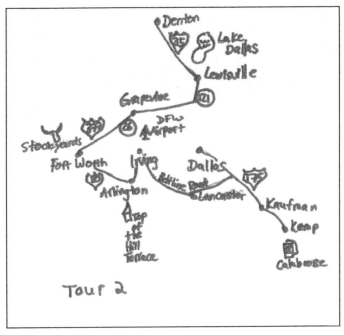

Tour 2 Routes

Dallas (see Tour 1) - Kaufman County - Kemp Calaboose - Lancaster Bank - Sowers Ambush - Top'o'the Hill Terrace - Fort

Worth Stockyards - Grapevine Calaboose and Dove Road - Lewisville Bank - Downtown Denton

Kaufman County
US 175, TX 34, and TX 243
Kaufman, Texas
Directions:
1) Kaufman is approximately 33 miles southeast of Dallas.
2) From downtown Dallas, take US 175 southeast to Kaufman. US 175 is called C.F. Hawn Freeway as it passes through South Dallas.
What's to See:
Not much of old Kaufman remains – both the courthouse and jail where Bonnie Parker spent a few weeks after a botched robbery in Kemp have been replaced with modern structures. However, the county poor farm, which was built in the 1880s and housed not only debtors but terminally ill people who couldn't afford medical care, is still visible on TX 34 (Mulberry Street) on the eastern side of town.

Bonnie and Ralph Fults spent an uncomfortable night at the Kemp Calaboose.
Photo by author.

Kemp Calaboose
Downtown Kemp
US 175, Kaufman County, Texas

Directions:
1) From Kaufman, take US 175 for 12 miles southeast to Kemp.
2) In Kemp, take Business US 175, which will bring you right into town.
3) Follow the signs to the Kemp downtown business district.
4) The sturdy calaboose still stands in its original location in an alley behind the southern side of Kemp's Main Street.

What's to See:
> After a botched hardware store robbery, Clyde fled and left Bonnie and his friend, Ralph Fults, to their own devices. Bonnie and Ralph were caught and locked up in the town's lone jail – a calaboose - a brick structure just in the back of the police station. After spending a very uncomfortable night, Bonnie was taken to the Kaufman County jail in Kaufman. Her mother refused to bail her out, hoping she'd come to her senses. Didn't work, did it?

Lancaster Bank (what's left of it)
Downtown Lancaster Square
TX 342 and South Belt Line Road
Dallas County, Texas

Directions:
1) From Kemp, follow US 175 northwest as if you're returning to Dallas.
2) At a small settlement in Dallas County called Kleburg, turn left (south) onto South Belt Line Road. Note that as you follow South Belt Line Road, it will change to North Belt Line Road, East Belt Line Road, and then West Belt Line Road.
3) Follow Belt Line Road to the southeast. Along this way, you will see very rural parts of Dallas County – Belt Line Road, Dallas' original loop highway, even becomes a two lane country road at one point.
4) Lancaster is located directly on Belt Line Road after you pass the Interstate 45 intersection.
5) To get to the Lancaster Square, take Dallas Road (TX 342) north.

What's to See:

Downtown Lancaster is very cute and walkable. The bank that Clyde and Raymond Hamilton robbed, located a block east off the downtown square, is now only a vacant lot, though the original flooring can still be seen (as of this writing). After this bank job, Clyde and Raymond split ways because Clyde believed Raymond had pocketed more than his fair share.

Sowers Ambush Site
Esters Road
Irving, Texas
Directions:
1) From downtown Lancaster, turn left (west) onto West Main Street to the intersection of West Main Street and West Belt Line Road.
2) Turn right (west) onto West Belt Line Road. West Belt Line Road is also FM 1382.
3) Drive for approximately 12 miles to the intersection where FM 1382 and West Belt Line Road veer to the northeast. At this intersection, West Belt Line Road becomes South Belt Line Road.
4) Make sure to veer to the northeast to follow South Belt Line Road / FM 1382.
5) Follow South Belt Line Road / FM 1382 (which will become North Belt Line Road once you pass Cedar Hill State Park) for approximately 18 miles to the intersection of TX 183/ West Airport Freeway.
6) At the intersection of Belt Line Road and TX 183 / West Airport Freeway, turn left onto the west feeder road of TX 183. Remain on the feeder road until it intersects with Esters Road.
7) Turn right (north) onto Esters Road.
What's to See:
As you travel through southern Dallas County, you will notice the large, chalky hills that belie the image that Dallas sits on a flat prairie. You will pass by Cedar Hill State Park (biking, camping, fishing,) and through downtown Grand Prairie. Near the busy intersection of TX 183 and Belt Line Road in Irving is the little town of Sowers, now completely swallowed by Home

Depot, Lowe's, and fast food restaurants, but once a rural, out-of-the-way settlement.

The failed ambush on Bonnie and Clyde, instigated by Dallas Sheriff Smoot Schmid, occurred at the intersection of Esters Road and TX 183 / West Airport Freeway, which was once known as the Fort Worth Turnpike. The site is located at one of the tallest hills in the county.

Top of the Hill Terrace
Arlington Baptist College
3001 Division Street
Arlington, Texas
Directions:
1) At the Sowers Ambush Site on Esters Road in Irving, take the Esters Road bridge south over TX 183 / West Airport Freeway.
2) Turn left (east) onto the TX 183/ West Airport Freeway feeder road.
3) At the intersection of TX 183/ West Airport Freeway feeder road and Belt Line Road, turn right (south) onto Belt Line Road.
4) Follow Belt Line Road south approximately 6 miles to TX 180 / Main Street in Grand Prairie.
5) Turn right (west) onto TX 180 / Main Street and continue west for approximately 6 miles to downtown Arlington.
6) Note that while you want to continue to follow TX 180, the street changes names along the way. In Arlington, TX 180 becomes Division Street.
7) Follow TX 180 / Division Street west from downtown Arlington until you see a simple globe with "ABC" – Arlington Baptist College - painted on it on your right.
8) Drive through the sandstone gates of Arlington Baptist College and follow the signs on campus to visitor's parking.

The guardhouse at Top of the Hill Terrace, a former speak-easy. Photo by author.

What's to See:

TX 180 is the original road that connected Dallas to Fort Worth. Paved and improved in the 1920s, the road is also known as the Bankhead Highway and "Old US 80." As you drive down this grand old highway, you will pass through downtown Arlington (on Division Street), where US 80 intersected with the ancient Texas Military Road at what is now Center Street.

Many of the buildings and houses you'll encounter along this highway will be the same that Bonnie and Clyde saw as they drove this road so many years ago.

The quiet campus of the Arlington Baptist College used to be a lot more active. During the late 1920s, this place was known as the "Top of the Hill Terrace," a gambling and sporting saloon near the Arlington Downs Racetrack where the hoi polloi as well as Dallas and Fort Worth's shady characters liked to hang out. It is not known if Bonnie and Clyde ever frequented this place, but because this was a speakeasy during Prohibition, they may have felt safe enough from the laws to grab a quick bite to eat and something to drink.

Many of the original sandstone structures left over from when the place was a speakeasy are used by the college. Under the campus book store is an escape tunnel, which patrons would use during raids.

Fort Worth Stockyards Hotel
Fort Worth Stockyards National Historic District
109 East Exchange Avenue
Fort Worth, Texas
Directions:
1) From the gates of Arlington Baptist College, turn right (west) onto Division Street to go towards Handley.
2) Note that Division Street's name changes to Lancaster Avenue in Handley.
3) Continue to follow Lancaster Avenue west into Fort Worth.
4) In Fort Worth, turn right (north) onto Commerce Street.
5) Follow Commerce Street through downtown Fort Worth. Commerce Street will make a circle around the Tarrant County Courthouse.
6) On the Commerce Street Circle, stay to the right as Commerce Street turns into US 287 / North Main Street.
7) Follow US 287 / North Main Street to the intersection of North Main Street and East Exchange Avenue in the Fort Worth Stockyards National Historic District. There is no free parking in the Stockyards.
What's to See:

Goodness, what's not to see? The Fort Worth Stockyards can arguably be called the best-tourist-attraction-in-Texas-that-is-still-authentic. And, you can order Calf Fries at the steak houses.[101]

But let's focus on Bonnie and Clyde. First, the drive to the Stockyards goes through the heart of Fort Worth's underbelly – East Lancaster Avenue is still not the best address, and the area around the Convention Center used to be Fort Worth's notorious Hell's Half Acre. Up until the 1960s, bars, pawn shops, liquor stores, and topless venues turned profits here.

The Fort Worth Stockyards have become an international tourist attraction. Photo by author.

During the 1930s, the Stockyards weren't as clean and friendly as they seem now. Large slaughter houses churned out all sorts of meat products at the eastern end of the district, so millions of cattle, sheep, and pigs lined the pens. Cowboys, gamblers, outlaws, and businessmen partied, conducted trade, and slept here amid the noise and smells.

Bonnie and Clyde spent a night in room 305 at the Stockyards Hotel at the corner of North Main Street and Exchange Avenue. Supposedly, a gun belonging to Bonnie (a girl's pink pistol, maybe?) was found inside one of the bedrooms. Despite the provenance displayed in the room, this is still an unsubstantiated claim - but far be it from me to dispute Bonnie and Clyde rumors!

Grapevine Calaboose
Downtown Grapevine
TX 26, TX 121, TX 114
Tarrant County, Texas
Directions:
1) East Exchange Avenue is a one-way street. You will need to go back to North Main Street.
2) To get back to North Main Street from East Exchange Street, take East Exchange Street until it ends at Stockyards Boulevard.

3) Turn left (north) onto Stockyards Boulevard and follow it around until it intersects with North Main Street.

4) Turn right (north) onto North Main Street.

5) At the intersection of North Main Street and TX 183 / NE 28th Street, turn right (east) onto NE 28th Street.

6) Follow TX 183 / NE 28th Street for approximately 6 miles until it intersects with TX 183 / East Belknap Road in Haltom City.

7) Turn left (northeast) onto TX 183 / East Belknap Road. Follow this road for approximately 2 miles.

8) East Belknap Road will split into Boulevard 26 (northeast) and Baker Street (east). Take Boulevard 26 / Grapevine Highway northeast for approximately 16 miles to Main Street in Grapevine. You will pass through Colleyville and Southlake.

9) Note that in Colleyville, Boulevard 26 / Grapevine Highway becomes Colleyville Boulevard. In Southlake, Colleyville Boulevard becomes Ira E. Woods Avenue. Both of these roads are TX 26.

10) In Grapevine, turn left (north) onto Main Street. Free parking is relatively easy to find.

What's to See:

The Grapevine Highway is also a vintage road, but development has obliterated many of the older structures and landscapes. Grapevine itself, however, has become a very nice tourist center, with lots of shops and restaurants that try to maintain the historic village feel of the city. After all, Sam Houston held one of the first treaty signings between Texans and the Cherokees right here!

You'll find a rounded calaboose along the west (left) side of Grapevine's Main Street, where associates of Clyde's were once jailed (the calaboose was originally located behind the police station, but was moved to become a tourist attraction).

The Gaylord Texan at Grapevine (1501 Gaylord Trail), a massive hotel and conference center, was built over an alleged Barrow Gang hideout.

Easter Sunday Murder Site
Dove Road and TX 114

Grapevine, Texas
Directions:
1) From downtown Grapevine, take Main Street north to TX 114/ Northwest Highway.
2) Turn left (west) onto TX 114/ Northwest Highway. Follow TX 114 / Northwest Highway for approximately 7 miles. After about 2 miles, you will merge right (northwest) onto the TX 114 freeway.
3) Take the Dove Road Exit and turn right onto Dove Road. The site of the murders is in the vicinity of TX 114 and Dove Road and is commemorated by a granite marker on the right (south) side of Dove Road.
What's To See:
Near the intersection of Dove Road and TX 114, Clyde and Henry Methvin killed two motorcycle troopers, Edward Bryan Wheeler and H.D. Murphy, on Easter Sunday, 1934. Due to rapid development, the area does not look like it did in the 1930s, though as of this writing, there are still patches of nature surrounding the site. Parking around the handsome granite marker memorializing the victims is difficult, so take caution.

First National Bank of Lewisville (now a restaurant and bar)
165 West Main Street
Lewisville, Texas
Directions:
1) From Dove Road and TX 114, turn back southeast on TX 114.
2) Follow TX 114 southeast. It will merge with TX 121.
3) By Dallas Fort Worth International Airport, TX 114 and TX 121 split. Follow TX 121 north, which will take you away from the airport.
4) Continue north on TX 121. In Lewisville, you will take the Business TX 121 exit (to the right).
5) Follow TX 121 north into Lewisville. You will pass under the Interstate 35 bridge.
6) Immediately after the Interstate 35 bridge, turn left (northwest) onto South Mill Street.
7) Dive north on South Mill Street to College Street in downtown Lewisville.

8) Turn left onto College Street (one way towards the west) and remain in the left lane. Follow College Street as it loops around downtown and merges with Main Street (one way towards the east) on the west side of downtown.

What's to See:

In 1934, Raymond Hamilton committed his last crime when he robbed the First National Bank of Lewisville, which was located on the bottom floor of a two-story building on the north side of downtown at the intersection of Main and Podyras Streets. Today, this former bank is a restaurant and bar.

When Raymond left the scene, he did so by following US 77 (Mill Street) north. If you drive north on Mill Street today, you'll end up in Lake Lewisville – the old highway was drowned when Lake Dallas was expanded in 1948.

At the intersection of Main and Kealy Streets is Tierney's Café, which is located in what used to be the town doctor's residence. The doctor supposedly was kidnapped, blindfolded, and brought to the Barrow Gang's hideout at Lake Dallas to treat their wounds.

The Texas movie premier of *Bonnie and Clyde* occurred at the Campus Theater in Denton. Photo by author.

Downtown Denton
US 77, US 377, and Hickory Streets
Denton County, Texas
Directions:

(The last leg of your trip through the greater Dallas Fort Worth Area will actually involve – gasp! – the Interstate. Since Lake Lewisville effectively cuts off Lewisville from the rest of Denton County, the easiest way to get to the county seat is to take Interstate 35 north from Lewisville.)

1) From Main Street in downtown Lewisville, turn left (north) onto North Mill Street.

2) Turn left (west) onto College Street (one way towards the west). Remain on the right side of the road.

3) Veer onto West Main Street and follow it to the Interstate 35 E intersection.

4) Take North Interstate 35 E for approximately 15 miles towards Denton.

5) In Denton, take the US 377 / Fort Worth Drive exit.

6) Turn right (north) onto Fort Worth Drive.

7) Fort Worth Drive will split into a "Y." Follow the left path of the "Y," where Fort Worth Drive becomes South Carroll Boulevard.

8) Follow South Carroll Boulevard north to the intersection of South Carroll Boulevard and West Hickory.

9) Turn right (east) onto West Hickory (one way towards the east) and follow that street to downtown Denton. Free parking is available all around the square.

What's to See:

As you wind your way to Denton, you'll pass the lakeside city of Lake Dallas, where Clyde and his fellow gang-members hid out from the law (their camp site is most likely under Lake Lewisville now). On West Hickory Street near downtown Denton sits the Campus Theater with its lovely neon sign. Today, community art councils and university students perform plays here, but in 1967 the theater hosted the premier of the movie, *Bonnie and Clyde.*

Denton was also the site of Clyde's first real crime – robbing a safe from a gas station – but the original gas station, which used to be right behind the Campus Theater on Oak Street, has been replaced by a non-descript office building. The Barrow Gang supposedly tried to rob the Denton First National Bank (today's Wells Fargo building, at the southeast corner of the square), but decided against it when they discovered that downtown was swarming with police cars, as it was court day.

The First State Bank in Ponder, Denton County, Texas. Photo by author.

Many small towns in Denton County - Justin, Ponder, Pilot Point - also served as location spots for the movie. Above is Ponder's First State Bank. In the movie scene, Clyde, wanting to impress Bonnie, tries to rob the bank but finds out that it was bankrupt. In reality, it was Raymond Hamilton who attempted to rob a closed-down bank.

Tour 3 – The Biographical Trip
Dallas, Texas to Arcadia, Louisiana (2 days).

A real "meat and potatoes" tour of Bonnie and Clyde, this tour takes you from cradle to grave. Although the couple drove all over the Southwest and Midwest during their short lives, they died a mere three hours away from Dallas.

This trip can be as short or long as you wish, as you can take one day to explore Dallas and then drive over to Louisiana for more "site seeing." The best part about this trip is that you don't have to do the entire itinerary together.

You will be following US 80 for the most part. Although Interstate 20 has now bypassed US 80, remember that dedicated road trippers eschew the Interstate - except if there's no other choice, of course!

All directions originate from Dallas.

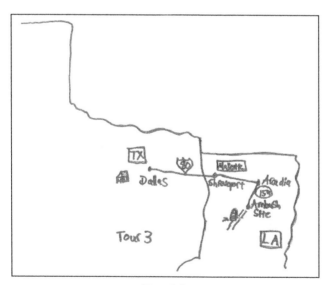

Tour 3 Routes

Dallas (see Tour 1) - US 80 - Shreveport: Pano's Diner – Gibsland - Arcadia

US 80

Old US Highway that linked Georgia to California
Dallas, Texas to Shreveport, Louisiana (190 miles)
Directions:
1) From downtown Dallas, take Interstate 30 east to exit 54, which is the exit to US 80.
2) Veer right onto US 80 east and head towards Terrell.
3) Keep east on US 80 all the way to Marshall.
4) After Marshall, US 80 will veer onto Interstate 20 for a short while.
5) To continue on US 80, take exit 633 at Waskom and follow US 80 east over the state line.
6) Outside of Shreveport, Louisiana, US 80 will share the road with US 79 and will be called Greenwood Road all the way to downtown Shreveport, where it becomes Texas Avenue.
What's to See:

US 80, commissioned in 1926, is a vintage Bonnie and Clyde road. They traveled this road quite a bit, as they sometimes spent the night at the home of Emma Parker's relatives near Longview. You'll be passing through the downtown areas of several lovely east Texas towns, such as Mineola (lots of antique stores) and Marshall (old neon signs and a beautiful courthouse just south of US 80). Jefferson, the seat of Marion County about twenty miles north of Marshall on US 59, is chock full of antebellum architecture and at least one plantation house.

Waskom, a Texas town on US 80 very close to the Louisiana border, was the site of a murder committed by one-time Barrow associate Joe Palmer. He killed Wade McNabb, a former fellow prison inmate, whom he believed to be a police informant. Joe Palmer was later executed in Huntsville on the same day as Raymond Hamilton.

What was once the Majestic Café in Shreveport. Photo by author.

Pano's Diner
422 Milam Street
Shreveport, Louisiana
Directions:
1) Once in Shreveport, continue east on US 80/US 79/ Greenwood Road, which becomes Texas Avenue after the Interstate 20 overpass.
2) Continue following Texas Avenue to the intersection of Cotton Street, where Texas Avenue becomes a one way street in the opposite direction.
3) Veer right (east) onto Cotton Street.
4) Turn left (north) onto LA 3036 / Common Street.
5) After three blocks, turn right (east) onto US 80 / Texas Street. Continue east on Texas Street in downtown Shreveport.
6) In downtown Shreveport, turn right (south) onto Spring Street.
7) Turn right (west) onto Milam Street (one way towards the west). Pano's Diner will be on your right.
What's to See:
　　You will definitely recognize that you're in the South once you drive through Shreveport. Shotgun houses, cotton exchanges, and magnolia trees line the road. Shreveport lies directly on the Red River, and came about due to the clearing of

a large log jam by Captain Henry Shreve in the 1830s, which allowed the Red River to be navigable above Natchitoches. Steam-driven paddlewheel boats made Shreveport into a major shipping port, and several rail roads came through the town after the Civil War.

Today, with its glittering casinos, brick warehouses, and wrought-iron architecture, downtown Shreveport is a mix of old and new. The town experienced a building boom in the 1920s, so Art-Deco buildings abound. Pano's Diner occupies the ground floor of one of these buildings. A few days before the ambush, Henry Methvin supposedly ordered sandwiches for Bonnie, Clyde and himself at the Majestic Café, which is now Pano's Diner. While he waited on the order inside the restaurant, Bonnie and Clyde, who were sitting in the car, raced away upon spotting a police cruiser. Clyde's erratic driving roused suspicion, and the officers briefly chased the couple. When the police told the Texas Ambush Posse about their encounter, the stage was set for the ambush. However, Henry Methvin may have separated himself from Bonnie and Clyde on purpose to aid in the ambush.

Gibsland
Canfield's Café, now the Ambush Museum, and other businesses
2419 Main Street
Gibsland, Louisiana
Directions:
1) From Pano's Diner in downtown Shreveport, take Milam Street southwest (one way towards the southwest) to McNeil Street.
2) Turn right (north) onto McNeil Street (one way towards the north) and continue for one block.
3) Turn right (east) onto US 80 / US 71 / Texas Road and follow US 80 for approximately 46 miles to Gibsland.
4) US 80 intersects LA 154 / Main Street in Gibsland.
What's to See:
Bonnie bought her last meal from Ma Canfield's Café in Gibsland – a sandwich, which was found half-eaten on her lap after the ambush. Today, the old café is the Bonnie and Clyde Ambush Museum, a fun and informative museum dedicated to

the crime duo. Owned and operated by Charles Heard and Ken Holmes, Jr., a noted crime historian, the museum displays photos, guns, the 1967 movie car, and houses a research archive. Other businesses along Main Street provide information about the ambush as well. A kind of party atmosphere permeates Gibsland, which gets even more pronounced every year around May 23, when Gibsland hosts the Bonnie and Clyde Festival, complete with reenactments.

No, this is not a grave, but the marker commemorates what put Bonnie and Clyde in theirs. Photo by author.

Ambush Site
Bienville Parish Historical Marker
LA 154 South between Mount Lebanon and Sailes
Bienville Parish, Louisiana
Directions:

1) From LA 154/ Main Street in Gibsland, continue south on LA 154 for about 3 miles to Mount Lebanon.

2) In Mount Lebanon, veer right (south) onto LA 154. Follow this road to an area called Pleasant Hill. I guess it wasn't that pleasant for Bonnie and Clyde! The ambush marker will be on the right side at the bottom of a long, shallow hill.

What's to See:

Upon leaving Gibsland on LA 154, note a dark, red brick building to your left. That's the former elementary school, where kids streamed out on the day of the ambush to gawk at the dead outlaws. On the way to the ambush marker, take a look at the antebellum dogtrot houses (dogtrots are houses with an open breezeway through the middle) in and around Mount Lebanon, a cute little village nestled in the Louisiana pine.

The ambush road does not look like it did when Bonnie and Clyde drove to their doom. LA 154 has been paved, has become wider, and the trees that once surrounded it have been trimmed away from the edges of the road. As you crest a small hill and make your way towards the ambush marker, you will need to use your imagination to picture what the highway looked like all those years ago.

Think about the ambush posse, consisting of Frank Hamer, Manny Gault, Bob Alcorn, Ted Hinton, Prentiss Oakley, and Henderson Jordan, hiding in the thickets, slapping at mosquitoes and smelling of cigarettes and stale coffee. Imagine Ivy Methvin's pick-up truck parked in the middle of the road, leaning crookedly on a jack. Listen for the sound of a new, very powerful Ford barreling down the road as if the driver was late to his appointment with hell.

The site where Bonnie and Clyde met their ends is commemorated by a large concrete slab that was erected by Bienville Parish. The marker is pocked with bullet holes and has been spray painted with graffiti. A number of small camp sites, with trash strewn about, surround the immediate vicinity. The marker feels almost like a pilgrimage site, but with SERIOUSLY disrespectful pilgrims.

The marker text reads:

"On this site May 23, 1934
Clyde Barrow
And
Bonnie Parker
Were killed by
Law Enforcement Officials"

That pretty much sums it up!

Arcadia

Conger Funeral Parlor and Furniture Store; Bienville Parish
Depot Museum
Railroad Street
Arcadia, Louisiana
Directions:
1) From the ambush marker, turn north to head back to Gibsland
on LA 154.
2) In Gibsland, turn right (east) onto US 80 / South 3rd Street.
Follow that road east for about 10 miles to Arcadia, Bienville
Parish's county seat.
3) In Arcadia, take US 80 / 2nd Street to North Beech Street.
4) Turn right (south) onto US 80 / North Beech Street.
5) Turn left (east) onto US 80 / 1st Street.
6) Turn right (south) onto Maple Street.
7) Turn left (east) onto Railroad Street. You'll find ample
parking along Arcadia's Antique Row.
What's to See:
After the ambush, the bullet-riddled car (with Bonnie and
Clyde still inside) was towed to the parish seat, Arcadia. The
bodies were laid out to be examined by the coroner at Conger's
Furniture Store, which, like in many small towns at the time,
doubled as a funeral home. Conger's Store today consists only of
a tiled floor – the building, damaged by wind and weather, is
long gone.
Across from Conger's Furniture Store and Funeral Parlor
is the wooden Bienville Depot, which has been turned into a
museum that displays many photos of the infamous day when
Arcadia became a town known around the world.

Downtown Arcadia has antique stores and restaurants to make your trip complete. Every month, Arcadia hosts Bonnie and Clyde Trade Days. These "trade days," which take place on the third weekend of each month, consist of a giant flea market and have nothing to do with Bonnie nor Clyde, but hey, they bring in the tourists.

Not much is left of the Conger Furniture Store and Funeral Home . Photo by author.

Tour 4 – The Legendary Trip
Dallas, Texas to Dexter, Iowa (2-3 days).

      Like Clyde Barrow, you will be driving a lot along this tour. The lure of speedy travel that the Interstate promises can be great on this trip, so remember the mantra: eschew the Interstate!

      Tour 4 is one of the most exciting of the tours because you'll visit so many of the places that made Bonnie and Clyde legendary - the shootout locations. As you drive down these long stretches of road, you'll also realize just how much driving Clyde could accomplish in a single day.

      As with the other tours, all directions originate from Dallas.

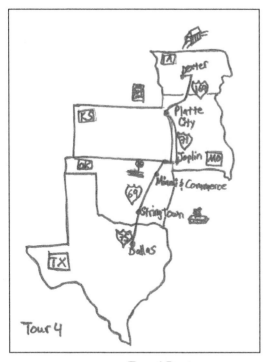

Tour 4 Routes

Dallas (see Tour 1) - Stringtown, Oklahoma – Miami and Commerce, Oklahoma - Joplin, Missouri - Dexter, Iowa.

The site of the dance hall shooting is now a fruit and vegetable stand. Photo by author.

Site of "Dance Hall Shooting"
US 69/US 75
Stringtown, Oklahoma
Directions:
1) From downtown Dallas, take US 75/US 69 north for approximately 80 miles into Oklahoma.
2) Follow US 69/ US 75 to the north, past Durant and Atoka, for approximately 53 miles. Stringtown is a little mining hamlet along US 69/US 75.
3) The shooting site will be on the west side of the road as you enter Stringtown from the south.
What's to See:

Stringtown, hometown of Reba MacEntire and a medium security prison, isn't the most cosmopolitan place now, and it wasn't back when Clyde, Raymond Hamilton, and Everett Mulligan decided to attend a country dance here in 1932. When two officers approached them, the gangsters shot them, killing Deputy Sheriff Eugene Moore. Today, the murder is commemorated by a granite state historical marker next to a small frame house that currently holds a fruit and vegetable stand. The dance took place on a platform where the green house now stands, and the shooting occurred near the platform.

Site of "Commerce Shooting"

US 69 (old US 66)

Miami (pronounced My-am-uh)and Commerce, Oklahoma

Directions:

1) From Stringtown, continue north on US 69 for approximately 217 miles. You will drive past the cities of Muskogee, Wagoner, and Vinita, Oklahoma.

2) US 69 (the old Route 66) becomes Miami's Main Street.

3) Continue north on US 69 to Commerce. You will find a small memorial honoring Cal Campbell on the right (east) side of US 69.

What's to See:

Miami is a beautiful, vibrant town that boasts one of the longest Route 66 Main Streets. Along Main Street, watch for the fabulous Coleman's Theater, a stunning vaudeville showplace in the Art Deco style, and several cafes, museums, and stores catering to the Route 66 traveler. Main Street is now US 69.

Follow US 69 north into Commerce, another vintage Route 66 town. Between the two towns are the Lost Trail and Crab Apple mines. It was near these mines where Clyde, Bonnie, and Henry Methvin parked along a dirt side road to take turns sleeping. As City Marshall Percy Boyd and Constable Cal Campbell came to investigate, Clyde shot Percy Boyd and took him hostage, while Henry Methvin shot and killed Cal Campbell. This proved to be the gang's last murder before their own demise a few weeks later in Louisiana.

Commerce commemorates the fallen constable with a sheltered plaque and a framed obituary in a small, roadside park along US 69 on the south side of town.

An original stretch of old Route 66 south of Miami. Photo by author.

Blast from the Past: Route 66

Before you get to Miami, take a trip through time on an original stretch of Route 66. On US 69 north of Narcissa and south of Miami, turn east (right) onto E140: you will find yourself on a narrow, concrete "ribbon road," which became US 66 after it had been paved in the 1920s. Though the landscape is still rural, a drive down this road will transport you back to the days of the Model T. Past many curves and dusty stretches (take extra precaution if it's raining), the road will lead to the fairgrounds in Miami. This original alignment meets up with Miami's Main Street, or US 69, north of the fairgrounds.

At the garage doors of this little apartment, two police officers were killed. Photo by author.

Joplin Mining Museum and the "Joplin Hideout"
Schifferdecker Park and 3347 ½ Oak Ridge Drive
MO 66, US 71, and Interstate 44
Joplin, Missouri
Directions:
1) From Commerce, Oklahoma, take US 69 north for 13 miles to Baxter Springs, Kansas. In Kansas, signs for US 69 to Baxter Springs may be posted as "Alt US 69".
2) Continue north of Baxter Springs, Kansas on Alt US 69 for approximately 6 miles north, then veer right (east) to follow KS 66/ 7th Street to Galena, Kansas.
3) Follow KS 66/7th Street through Galena and into Missouri. In Missouri, the road is designated as MO 66/ West 7th Street. Note that this is the route Bonnie and Clyde would have traveled, too.
4) Continue east on MO 66/ West 7th Street to downtown Joplin, Missouri.
5) The Joplin Mining Museum will be on your left hand side as you enter Joplin in a large outdoor recreation complex called Schifferdecker Park, an original rest stop on Old US 66. From MO 66/ West 7th Street, turn left onto Schifferdecker Avenue and follow the signs to the museum.

6) To continue to the "Joplin Hideout" from the Joplin Mining Museum, return to MO 66/ West 7th Street by turning left (east) at the intersection of Schifferdecker Avenue and MO 66/ West 7th Street.

5) Follow on MO 66/ West 7th Street to downtown Joplin, then turn right (south) on Main Street.

6) Continue south on Main Street for approximately 2 miles, then turn right (west) onto 32nd Street.

7) Turn left (south) on Oak Ridge Drive. The "Joplin Hideout," a garage apartment, sits behind the residence along a wide alley at 3347 Oak Ridge Drive.

What's to See:

Joplin is a large, busy city that has lead, zinc, and galena mining to thank for its existence. Clyde felt comfortable enough in Joplin to hide out for a while inside a garage apartment that had easy access for a quick get-a-way. Clyde, Bonnie, W.D. Jones, Buck Barrow, and Blanche Barrow rented this two bedroom flat in a middle-class neighborhood for about two weeks until their suspicious ways caught the laws' attention. While serving a search warrant, the gang fired on the police officers, killing Harry McGinnis and Wes Harryman.

The garage apartment, built of native stone with wooden framing, still stands in this hilly section of Joplin. While the interiors have been redone and the neighborhood has become quite gentrified, the scene is relatively unchanged from what occurred so many years ago. The current owners of the garage apartment rent out the rooms as a bed and breakfast, but there is a waiting list for those who want to book a room, so you'll need to make advance reservations (for more information, see the "Resource" section at the back of the book).

The Joplin Mining Museum Complex is a large museum with many exhibits and warrants a lengthy visit. The Bonnie and Clyde road tripper, however, should make a bee-line towards the back of the museum, where a display shows artifacts recovered from the Joplin Hideout. The original front door is mounted to the floor, though make sure to note that the holes in the door are not due to the famous shoot-out but are the result of a domestic disturbance that occurred years later. Also on display are two necklaces found among the many items in the apartment. That the museum even owns these artifacts is surprising in itself. Law enforcement officers, journalists, and curiosity seekers often took whatever they wanted during the confusion following the shoot-outs, and most of these items remain in the hands of their descendants and/or collectors to this day.

Platte City, Missouri
Kansas City, Red Crown Tourist Court, and Platte County Courthouse
US 71 and Interstate 435
Directions:
1) From downtown Joplin, take MO 43 / Main Street north for 3 miles to the Joplin Regional Airport. Then hop a plane to Kansas City. Hah! I'm kidding!
2) Turn right (east) onto MO 171/ DeMott Avenue south of the airport.
3) MO 171 will merge with US 71. Continue east on US 71/ MO 171 for approximately 10 miles until US 71/ MO 171 becomes a divided highway heading north.
4) Follow US 71 north for approximately 86 miles to Kansas City, Missouri. In Kansas City, US 71 is also called "Bruce R. Watkins Drive."
5) Continue driving north on US 71, onto which Interstates 35 and 29 will merge north of downtown, Kansas.
6) After downtown Kansas City, Missouri, follow US 71 north for approximately 34 miles, past the Kansas City International Airport, to Platte City, Missouri.
7) In Platte City, take the Main Street exit and head left (west) on Main Street to downtown Platte City.
What's to See:
Kansas City was a notorious place in the 1930s – it's where Pretty Boy Floyd ambushed four police officers and their prisoners in 1933 (the "Kansas City Depot Job," as Bonnie poetically explained) – and Bonnie and Clyde probably visited the gambling halls and speakeasies in the notorious West Bottoms.

After Bonnie was hurt in the Wellington, Texas, crash, Clyde, Bonnie, Buck, Blanche, and W.D. Jones stayed at the Red Crown Tourist Court just south of Platte City to help nurse her wounds. During a devastating gun battle between the Barrow Gang and local police that drastically changed the dynamic of the gang, Blanche sustained eye injuries from flying glass and Buck was shot in the head. The Red Crown Tourist Court and Tavern were built to look like castles and remained popular hang-outs in Platte City well into the 1960s. A fire destroyed the buildings and today, no trace of them remains. The buildings were located at the junctions of US 71 and US 59, which is now an empty field across from the Kansas City International Airport.

A decade or so ago, some enterprising souls had managed to salvage bricks from the court and sell them to tourists, so bits and pieces of the Red Crown are still floating around.

After the battle at Dexfield Park, Iowa (just a few days after the Red Crown Shootout), Blanche Barrow was arrested and taken to the Platte County jail that once stood behind the courthouse in Platte City. The jail has also been demolished. In its place stands the courthouse annex.

Platte City is a very pretty town situated on relatively steep hills. The town's museum just west of the square at 220 Ferrel Street is inside a Victorian brick mansion and has a large Civil War collection.

The Jesse James House Museum in St. Joseph even has authentic wall paper stains! Photo by author.

Blast from the Past: The Wild West
Directions:
1) From downtown Platte City, take Main Street east to return to US 71.
2) Take US 71 north to St Joseph, Missouri.
What's to See:

St. Joseph has an extensive Wild West heritage. Situated on a series of hills beside the wide and beautiful Missouri River, St. Joseph was considered a frontier town during the Civil War. The Pony Express began its legendary service here, and the stables are now a fun and interpretive museum at 914 Penn Street in downtown St. Joseph. The house where Jesse James was shot sits just a few blocks east of the Pony Express Museum at the intersection of Penn Street and 12th Street (behind the Patee House Museum). Not only are the furnishings original and the bullet hole is visible, but remains of Jesse's casket and a cast of his skull are on display as well. Strange, but true.

A neon sign greets the visitor to Dexter, Iowa. Photo by author.

Dexter, Iowa
Dexfield Park, site of Buck and Blanche Barrow's surrender
Maple Road (P 48) north of Dexter
Directions:
1) If you visited St. Joseph: From downtown St. Joseph, take US
59 / St Joseph Avenue north to Savannah Road. Turn right onto
Savannah Road, the turn right (east) onto Cook Road. Turn left
(north) onto US 169/ Rochester Road and follow it north for
approximately 115 miles to Interstate 80 in Iowa.
2) If you did not visit St. Joseph: Continue north on US 71. Take
the US 169/ Rochester Road exit. Follow US 169/ Rochester
Road north for approximately 115 miles to Interstate 80 in Iowa.
3) Take Interstate 80 west for 10 miles west to Dexter, Iowa.
Dexter lies on the "White Pole Road," which was built in 1910 as
a state-of-the-art highway linking Des Moines to Council Bluffs.
In Dexter, the "White Pole Road" is known as State Road, or F
65.

4) In Dexter, take Maple Road (P48) to the right (north). After approximately 8 miles, you will see two markers on the west (left) side of the road, next to the Raccoon River. This is the old Dexfield Park.

5) Alternately, you can take Interstate 35 from Kansas City to Des Moines, then Interstate 80 west to Dexter. That is, if you refuse to meander, but... isn't meandering the whole point of a road trip?

What's To See:

The drive from St. Joseph, Missouri to Dexter, Iowa is beautiful and peaceful with little traffic. In Iowa, US 169 will take you through Winterset, the seat of Madison County, so watch out for the covered bridges that may make you fall in love with the nearest photographer or Italian housewife, depending on your preference. (This was a reference to the book, *The Bridges of Madison County,* by Robert James Waller, and the sappy movie of the same name. Yes, bad jokes abound in this book.)

Dexter was tiny in the 1930s, and it still is today. The town was once a lot busier when Dexfield Park was still in operation. The park, which opened in 1915, had a cement swimming pool, diving board, picnic grounds, petting zoo, hiking trails, and canoe rentals.

When the Barrow Gang, badly wounded after the shootout at the Red Court Tourist Camp in Platte City, decided to hide out in the woods near the Raccoon River, Dexfield Park had already been closed for a few years. The abandoned amusement park offered the gang plenty of advantages: the fields were still relatively clear, but the underbrush offered good cover; small trails made a quick get-a-way easier; and the location by the river provided a good water source.

As word spread about the gang, an ambush posse was formed, and the party surprised the gang in the early morning of July 24, 1933. Clyde, Bonnie, and W.D. Jones were able to shoot their way out. Buck, who had sustained a head wound during the Platte City shoot-out, and Blanche, whose eyes had been hurt by flying glass when the car's window was struck, were left behind. Blanche surrendered and was taken into custody. Buck was brought to the King's Daughters Hospital in Perry, where he died a few days later (Perry is located north on US 169 to Iowa State Highway 141 west). The hospital is now the Perry Lutheran Home, located at 2323 East Willis Avenue.

Today, Dexfield Park is remembered only by a granite marker on the west side of the Raccoon River. Plowed fields have replaced the swimming pool, and a private farm stands now on the site where the shoot-out took place. Raccoon River, which Bonnie, Clyde, and W.D. crossed to escape the posse, runs swiftly towards the east. Wounded and resting along the Raccoon River bank, Bonnie had asked W.D. to shoot her if Clyde didn't return after he had set off to steal another automobile.

One of the banks the Barrow Gang robbed is in Stuart, a small town to the west of Dexter (take White Pole Road/ IA 925 west). The building proudly displays its association with the robbers, even though it is now home to a police station!

Some Bonnie and Clyde researchers maintain that Dexfield Park proved to be the gang's Waterloo. The gun fight was definitely a turning point, as Buck died, Blanche was sent to prison, and W.D. Jones deserted the gang. Clyde had to find new gang members to continue his path of destruction, which led to the Eastham Raid and ultimately, his own demise.

The road trip throughout the Midwest shows how Bonnie and Clyde's travels made them "legendary." Clyde's most vicious killings took place along these stretches, and his driving endurance can be seen just by the distances he could put behind him in a single day. Not a lot has changed in many of the stops along this trip, making the Bonnie and Clyde experience that much more real.

Tour 5 – The Informative Trip(s)
All over the place! (Whenever you have some time).

If you like day trips or short overnight trips, this tour will fit your bill. Along these roads, you will be going far and wide. But you will also have the chance to see some true southwestern scenery!

The trips on this tour are not interconnected and need not be taken in sequence. The destinations are arranged in alphabetical order by location. All directions originate from Dallas.

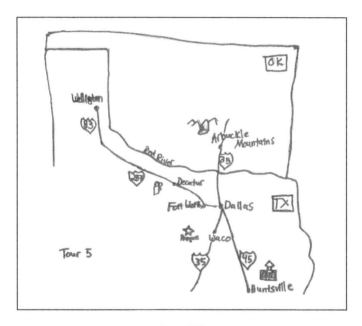

Tour 5 Routes

Arbuckle Mountains, Oklahoma - Decatur, Texas (Texas Tourist Camp) - Huntsville, Texas (Walls Unit, Texas Prison Museum, Eastham Prison, Prison Graves) - Waco, Texas (Ranger Museum, jail) - Wellington, Texas (Salt Fork of the Red River Bridge)

Abandoned tourist courts and souvenir shops abound on US 77 in the Arbuckle Mountains. Photo by author.

Arbuckle Mountains
US 77
Between Springer and Davis, Oklahoma
Directions:
1) From Dallas, take US 77/Interstate 35 north for approximately 126 miles into Oklahoma.
2) Take Exit 1 – Thackerville to follow US 77 north for approximately 45 miles.
3) After passing through Marietta, Ardmore, and Springer, Oklahoma, you will notice a gradual uplift until suddenly, you are in the Arbuckle Mountains, one of the most interesting small ranges in all of North America, according to geologists. (They say that the Arbuckle mountains have some of the easiest rock to "read." I'll take their word for it.)
What's to See:
As US 77 winds around the Arbuckle Mountains between Springer and Davis, the vista becomes increasingly breathtaking. A scenic overlook at the top of a mountain offers a beautiful view of the valley where Turner Falls empties into Honey Creek. The falls, which at 70 feet are the highest waterfalls in

Oklahoma, can be visited at the bottom of US 77 inside a park owned by the city of Davis. Two deep and clear swimming holes, the ruins of a castle, tourist cabins, souvenir shops, artists in residence, and even tipi lodges give the visitor the experience of being in a kind of time warp, when vacations were family-oriented, kitschy, and didn't have to involve major travel to be fun.

Along the road toward Davis, many other remnants of the Arbuckle Mountain's tourist days are still visible, including long abandoned tourist courts, cabin ruins, metal outlines of old neon signs, and even a defunct amusement park.

Bonnie, Clyde, and D.W. Jones hid out in these mountains and may have stayed in one of the tourist camps that used to line US 77. In any case, they would have felt right at home here because this stretch of highway was built by prison labor in the late 1920s.

Decatur, Texas
Texas Tourist Camp
Corner of Hale Avenue and Business US 81
Directions:
1) From Dallas, take Interstate 35 E north to Denton.
2) In Denton, take US 380 west for 25 miles to Decatur.
3) From US 380 in Decatur, veer left (southwest) onto Business 380.
4) Turn left (south) at the intersection of Business 380 and South Business US 81. Follow South Business US 81 to the south. The Texas Tourist Camp will be on your right where Hale Avenue intersects South Business US 81.
-Or-
1) From Dallas, take Interstate 30 west to Fort Worth
2) In Fort Worth, take Interstate 35 W north to Rhome, Texas.
3) In Rhome, go north on US 287 to Decatur.
4) In Decatur, take the South Business 81 exit and head north into town.
5) The Texas Tourist Camp will be on your left at the intersection of Hale Avenue and South Business 81.
What's to See:

Bonnie and Clyde supposedly stayed at this tourist camp, and it's not a stretch to understand that claim. The tourist court and gas station, the first of its kind in Decatur, was built in 1927 right alongside US 81 (which parallels the old Chisholm Trail). Each cabin had a garage, an important feature for Clyde who'd want to hide his stolen car, and the garages all faced a busy intersection of state highways.

Cabin at the Texas Tourist Camp offered all the amenities Clyde Barrow looked for – proximity to highways and a garage. Photo by author.

The gas station was built with petrified wood, which was found in the vicinity. In later years, the owners faced the cabins with the same petrified wood to give them a distinctive look, and also added a café. Today, the Texas Tourist Camp is a tourist attraction in its own right.

Decatur also has many other things to see, such as its beautiful red sandstone courthouse; the old Baptist College building, now the Wise County Museum; and the Waggoner Mansion, a neglected Victorian stone house where the owners of the Waggoner ranching empire used to hold family feuds. For the nature lover, the Lyndon B. Johnson National Grasslands are close by.

Bonnie and Clyde pistol.
This pistol was taken from the "death car". It was brought back to Texas and given to Lee Simmons.

A pistol, taken from Bonnie after her death, is displayed at the Texas Prison Museum. Photo by author.

Huntsville, Texas
Texas Prison Museum, Walls Unit, Captain Joe Bird Cemetery and Eastham Prison Farm
TX 75 or Interstate 45
Directions:
From Dallas, drive south on Interstate 45 for approximately 189 miles to Huntsville. (Directions to each attraction will follow).
What's To See:
   The *Texas Prison Museum* (take exit # 118; turn left (east) to SH 75 North) displays a gun taken from Bonnie's corpse after the ambush. Informative posters tell about the 1934 Eastham Prison Raid. And, as you round a corner, the wooden electric chair, nicknamed "Old Sparky," sits behind a three-walled partition. Used between 1924 and 1964, many a man – 361, actually - sizzled in this chair, including Barrow associates Raymond Hamilton and Joe Palmer.
   One of the better-run museums I've encountered, the Texas Prison Museum offers a well balanced look at the Texas prison system.
   The *Walls (or Huntsville) Unit* (turn right from the Prison Museum and follow TX 75 to 11th Street, turn left (east) onto 11th

Street, at downtown Huntsville take Avenue H south to 815 12th Street) is the oldest state prison in Texas. Dominating downtown Huntsville like a medieval fortress, the imposing, red brick Walls Unit was home to death row from 1928 to 1965 and also served the general prison population. The inmate infirmary was also located here.

Buck Barrow served his penance at the Walls Unit, and Clyde recuperated here after having his toes chopped off to get out of the Eastham Prison Farm. Clyde also made wooden jewelry boxes inside the Walls Unit, one of which he gave to his sister-in-law, Blanche Barrow.

Since the mid-nineteenth century, *Captain Joe Byrd Cemetery* (from 11th Street in downtown Houston, go east to Sycamore Drive, turn right (south), then turn left (east) onto Bowers Boulevard) has offered eternal rest for prisoners who died while in state custody and whose bodies were never collected by their next of kin. Kiowa Chief Satanta was once buried here, but his body was moved to the Fort Sill Cemetery for a more dignified burial. The stark white crosses in orderly rows only identify the dead by their prison numbers. Any grave marked with a discreet "X" means that the deceased was executed.

No Barrow associates are buried here, but the cemetery is a fascinating reminder of the grisly world of crime and punishment.

For historians of Clyde Barrow, the *Eastham Prison Farm* (take Bowers Boulevard east to Bearkat Boulevard, turn right (southeast), then turn left (north) onto TX 19 for 21 miles to Trinity, then turn left (west) onto FM 230/ Main Street, farm is thirteen miles west of Trinity) is a historic place indeed. Here, Clyde Barrow supposedly committed his first murder. Here, he turned into a "rattlesnake" under the back breaking labor and harsh treatment. Here, he had a fellow inmate cut off two toes in order to escape the work details. And here, Clyde staged a prison raid that freed several inmates, including Raymond Hamilton and Henry Methvin, which ultimately led to his own demise.

Because Eastham Prison Farm is still an active jail, visitors need special permission to enter the site. The actual barrack of the prison farm where Clyde slept is now just a shell, but still stands.

At the Texas Ranger Museum, make sure to visit the display on the so-bad-it's-good T.V. show, *Walker, Texas Ranger.* Photo by author.

Waco, Texas
Texas Ranger Museum and McLennan County Courthouse
100 Texas Ranger Trail
Directions:
From Dallas, take Interstate 35 for approximately 90 miles south to Waco. Directions to each attraction will follow.
What's to See:
The *Texas Ranger Museum* (Exit 335-B, University Parks, and follow signs) celebrates the heritage of Texas' oldest law enforcement organization with exhibits, archives, and a book store. The Barrow Gang Ambush permanent exhibit displays items taken from the bodies of Bonnie and Clyde (such as a pocket watch), weapons and license plates discovered in the death car, and documents supporting the ambush, including expense account reports.

Weeks after the ambush, Clyde and Bonnie's parents wrote to the Rangers, requesting that the items taken from the car be returned to them. That plea fell on deaf ears – the only items the family ever received were the clothes that the couple wore when they were killed.

The original *McLennan County Jail*, from which Clyde Barrow escaped in 1930 with Bonnie's help, is no longer standing, though a newer jail facility occupies the site. It is situated behind the beautiful *McLennan County Courthouse* at 501 Washington Avenue in downtown Waco (from Museum, take University Parks Drive north, then turn left (southwest) on Washington Avenue).

Wellington, Texas
"Red River Plunge" (actually Salt Fork of the Red River) and Collingsworth County Museum
US 83 north of Wellington, Texas
Directions:
1) From Dallas, take Interstate 30 west to Fort Worth.
2) In Fort Worth, take Interstate W north.
3) Take US 287 north at exit # 59.
4) Follow US 287 north/northwest for approximately 215 miles to Childress, Texas.
5) In Childress, turn right (north) onto US 83. Follow US 83 for approximately 24 miles north to Wellington.
6) The bridge spans the Salt Fork of the Red River a few miles north of Wellington on US 83.
What's to See:
This drive will take you through Wichita Falls, Electra, Vernon and Childress, towns where Clyde and his gang would occasionally hide out. West of Wichita Falls, you will be afforded breath taking views of the Caprock, a dramatic upwelling as the landscape enters the Llano Estacado, or Staked Plains, of the Texas Panhandle.

The new truss bridge, built after the crash, may have its days numbered. The bridge has become too narrow for traffic. Photo by author.

In Wellington, the multi-span, iron truss bridge that crosses over the Salt Fork did not exist in 1933. Driving at his usual high rate of speed, Clyde ignored the warning signs that the bridge had been washed out and ended up plunging into the river bottom. The Pritchards, whose farm was located on a bluff close by, witnessed the accident and tried to help the bandits. The daughter of the Pritchards was shot in the fingers by W.D. Jones for her efforts.

Across the river is a quiet camp site where cement bridge pillars still stand. Those pillars may be the old pilings of the road bridge, or could be remnants of a railroad bridge.

Note that the historical marker on US 83 commemorating the "plunge" is a little inaccurate. It mentions that Buck Barrow was with Bonnie and Clyde that night, but actually the third member was W.D. Jones.

The *Collingsworth County Museum* in downtown Wellington (824 East Avenue on the square in downtown Wellington) has pictures, newspaper articles, and artifacts pertaining to the Red River Plunge.

****

The many road trips that one can take to re-imagine Bonnie's and Clyde's lives not only bring the traveler to the source of all this history, but they also offer a glimpse into the not-so-distant past of an important epoch in American history. Though time has changed much of the landscapes and buildings drastically, certain tangible parts of history still linger around, just waiting to be discovered.

So what are you waiting for? Get in your car – on your bike – in a bus - and go exploring!

Epilogue

The exploits of Clyde Barrow and his various accomplices are fairly easy to research. Being in constant trouble with the law allowed Clyde's life to be chronicled very thoroughly – the proliferation of arrest warrants, police reports, trial transcripts, arraignment photographs, wanted posters, FBI files, and newspaper articles that Clyde left in his wake help to weave his history. Anecdotes from family members, acquaintances, gang members, and law enforcement officers, coupled with handy city directories, tax and deed records, help to fill in the gaps of time in his narrative. One could venture to say that Clyde Barrow's life was akin to an open book.

Yet, there's something of an enigma that surrounds Clyde Barrow and his girlfriend Bonnie Parker. They were two kids trapped in a horrendous economic depression with, apparently, no way out. Their parents barely made meager livings without much hope for improvement. The place where Bonnie and Clyde grew up, West Dallas, was an embarrassing bane to a city that prided itself on its progressive outlook. Even if Clyde and Bonnie had done nothing wrong, they lived under suspicion of the law, where lightly veiled hints of harassment and imprisonment became a constant threat merely because of who they were and where they lived.

But they could have "gone straight." They could have accepted living mediocre but respectable lives like their siblings, such as Clyde's sisters Artie and Nell or Bonnie's brother Buster. For some reason, though, Bonnie and Clyde decided early on that they were going to live on the edge and die that way. Maybe they wanted some kind of adventure; maybe they couldn't wait to buy the things that only money could give them; maybe they hated the status quo so much that they'd rather die than become part of it. They had forgiving families, street smarts, few scruples, and a desire to buck the system. Were they destined to become who they ended up being?

I've slowly discovered that fame has a consistent dark undercurrent, and that undercurrent is present whether the famous person is a talented actor or an unconscionable criminal. To court fame and notoriety, one must delve into the dark recesses of human nature, venture into seedy alley ways, deal with shady characters, and often debase ones values - all to get ahead. Sometimes, this walk on the dark side pays off, and fame and fortune are the rewards. Many more times, however, the walk leads straight into the abyss, where death and destruction await. Like Bonnie wrote, that kind of road gets dimmer and dimmer, so that one can hardly see where it's going, although everyone knows where it will end.

This book retraces that road. Luckily for us, that road is now a lighted path, where history, mythology, geography, and destiny intertwine.

Resources and Bibliography

Books and Articles Sourced and Recommended about Bonnie and Clyde

Ambush: The Real Story of Bonnie and Clyde by Ted Hinton as told to Larry Grove (Dallas: Southwestern Historical Publications, 1979).

    This retelling of the stakeout, and eventual ambush, of Clyde Barrow and Bonnie Parker is controversial, but offers wonderful insights into the way law enforcement worked in the 1930s.

Assignment Huntsville: Memoirs of a Texas Prison Official by Lee Simmons (Austin: University of Texas Press, 1957).

    Simmons' book was one of the first to expose the Methvin family's culpability in the Bonnie and Clyde ambush, and offers an insider look at the Eastham State Prison Farm Raid (or "rescue," as Emma Parker put it).

Bonnie and Clyde: A Twenty-First Century Update by James R. Knight with Jonathan Davis (Austin: Eakin Press, 2003).

    This book is an excellent, easy-to-read, foot-noted, well researched compendium on Bonnie and Clyde, with many never-before seen photographs and new stories uncovered. The authors also devote space to the Bonnie and Clyde harboring trial, which other chroniclers have overlooked.

I'm Frank Hamer: The Life of a Texas Peace Officer by John H. Jenkins and H. Gordon Frost (Austin: State House Press, 1968).

    A grandiose retelling of Frank Hamer's life, this biography paints Hamer in an almost saintly light. The stories in this book aren't always the most reliable, however.

My Life with Bonnie and Clyde by Blanche Caldwell Barrow, edited by John Neal Phillips (Norman: University of Oklahoma Press, 2004).

Blanche Barrow's memoirs add an entirely new – and often juicier – perspective on Bonnie and Clyde. Extensively foot-noted, this book is a great read.

On the Trail of Bonnie and Clyde: Then and Now by Winston G. Ramsey (Essex: After the Battle, 2003).

The author, an English Bonnie and Clyde aficionado, goes back to the places where Bonnie and Clyde hid out and chronicles the locations. A great snapshot of how the American historical and geographical landscapes have changed, this is not a travelogue but a pictorial reenactment of the Barrow Gang. (Note: *After the Battle Publications* is an excellent resource of then/now books, many of which focus on battle fields of World War II).

"Riding with Bonnie and Clyde: The Real-Life Model for C.W. Moss tells it like it was." W.D. Jones. *Playboy Magazine*, November 1968, 151, 160-165.

W.D. Jones wrote about his time with Bonnie and Clyde in a folksy, engaging style.

Running with Bonnie and Clyde: The Ten Fast Years of Ralph Fults by John Neal Phillips (Norman: University of Oklahoma Press, 1996).

Considered the most authoritative work on Bonnie and Clyde, Phillips delved into the history of the Barrow gang by interviewing a former gang member.

The Lives and Times of Bonnie and Clyde by E.R. Milner (Carbondale, Illinois: Southern Illinois University Press, 1996).

Milner, a professor of history, offers a more intellectual treatment of the crime duo.

*The True Story of Bonnie and Clyde as Told by Bonnie's Mother and Clyde's Sister, Mrs. Emma Parker and Mrs. Nell Barrow Cowan (*former title*: Fugitives)* by Jan Fortune (New York: Signet Books, 1968.)

This true-crime genre book is the first book most Bonnie and Clyde researchers use, though there are some errors, and some names were changed/omitted to protect the not-so-innocent.

The Strange History of Bonnie and Clyde by John Treherne (New York: Cooper Square Press, 1984).
A psychological study of the weirdness that was Bonnie and Clyde's relationship, this book is more conversational than it is academic.

Recommended and Sourced Websites

Frank Ballinger's Texas Hideout:
> http://texashideout.tripod.com/bc.htm

Ballinger's site is incredibly detailed and is constantly updated with new information, including excerpts from original newspaper articles about the gang, vintage photographs, and family histories. This website is a must-read for any Bonnie and Clyde searcher.

Henry Methvin:
> http://www.tmethvin.com/henry

This site is an excellent and well-documented account of Henry Methvin's life and crimes, with plenty of photos, primary sources, and links.

Blanche Caldwell Barrow:
> http://blanchebarrow.com

Deborah Moss, Blanche's cousin, authored a fun and respectful site for Blanche Barrow, with photos, memoires, resources, and really great music.

Museum and Such

Bienville Depot Museum
Free admission, free parking.
2440 Hazel Street
Arcadia, Louisiana 71001
http://www.arcadialouisiana.org/museums.htm

Bonnie and Clyde Ambush Museum
Admission charged, free parking, buses welcome.
2419 Main Street
Gibsland, Louisiana 71028
318-843-1934
http:// bonnieandclydemuseum.com

Collingsworth County Museum
Free admission, free parking.
PO Box 495, Wellington, TX 79095
806-447-5327
http://www.collingsworthcountymuseum.org/news.htm

Fort Worth Stockyards National Historical District
Free admission to Stockyards, parking fees, admissions fees
where applicable.
Exchange Avenue and Main Street
Fort Worth, Texas 76164
817-626-7921
http://www.fortworthstockyards.org/

Joplin Hideout Bed and Breakfast
Reservations required, free parking.
3347 ½ Oak Ridge Drive
Joplin, MO 64801
417-529-4664
http://www.joplinhideout.com

Joplin Mining Museum
Admission charged, free parking.

504 S Schifferdecker Ave
Joplin, Missouri 64801
417-623-1180

Old Red Courthouse Museum
Admission charged, parking fees.
100 South Houston St.
Dallas, TX 75202
214-745-1100
http://www.oldred.org/

Platte City Historical Society and Museum
Admission charged, free parking.
220 Ferrel Street
Platte City, MO 64079
http://www.rootsweb.ancestry.com/~mopchgs/

Texas Prison Museum
Admission charged, free parking.
491 SH 75 North
Huntsville, Texas 77320
http://www.txprisonmuseum.org/

Texas Ranger Museum and Hall of Fame
Admission charged, free parking.
100 Texas Ranger Trail
Waco, Texas 76706
254-750-8631
http://www.texasranger.org/

Cities and Such

Arcadia, Louisiana Official Webpage:
        http://www.arcadialouisiana.org
Dallas, Texas Convention and Visitor's Bureau:
        http://www.visitdallas.com/visitors
Denton, Texas Visitor's Guide:
        http://www.discoverdenton.com

Dexter, Iowa Community Website:
   http://www.dexteriowa.org
Fort Worth, Texas Visitor's Bureau:
   http://www.fortworth.com
Grapevine, Texas Convention and Visitor's Bureau:
   http://www.grapevinetexasusa.com
Joplin, Missouri Convention and Visitor's Bureau:
   http://www.joplincvb.com
Kansas City, Missouri Convention and Visitor's Bureau:
   http://www.visitkc.com
Kaufman, Texas Official City Website:
   http://www.kaufmantx.org
Lancaster, Texas Chamber of Commerce:
   http://www.lancastertx.org
Platte City, Missouri Official Website:
   http://www.plattecity.org
Shreveport, Louisiana Visitor's Guide:
   http://www.shreveport-bossier.org
Waco, Texas Convention and Visitor's Bureau:
   http://www.wacocvb.com

Other Sources

Dallas Historical Society:
   http://www.dallashistory.org
Louisiana Historical Society:
   http://www.louisianahistoricalsociety.org/links.htm

Index

Shameless Self Promotional Page

For the Road Tripper who doesn't have everything just yet....
Check out the other titles in the Traveling History series!

Traveling History Up the Cattle Trails: A Road Tripper's Guide to the Cattle Roads of the Southwest

Traveling History Amongst the Ghosts: A Road Tripper's Guide to Ghost Towns in the Red River Valley

Traveling History With Bonnie and Clyde: A Road Tripper's Guide to Gangster Sites in Middle America

Come join the great people who make their vacations into adventurous, fun, and informative road trips!

Contact

Red River Historian Press
Robin Cole Jett
101 Montego Bay
Lewisville, TX 75067
972-353-4130
robin@redriverhistorian.com

To book presentations and order the Traveling History Guides, or just to discover more stories, photos, and fun stuff, visit

http://www.redriverhistorian.com

[1] The Trinity River was unpredictable – in 1908, the river flooded so badly that Dallas was cut off from Oak Cliff for months as several bridges washed away. Throughout the 20th century, large engineering projects straightened out the river channel through a series of levees, but the Trinity still floods from time to time.

[2] Today's West Dallas is still an economically depressed area, though it's home to more Hispanics and African Americans than Southern whites. When the area was incorporated in 1952, Dallas renamed many of the streets to celebrate the city's movers and shakers, with the effect that West Dallas lost some of its distinctiveness. For example, Eagle Ford Road, named after one of the earliest settlements in Dallas County and the street on which Clyde lived, was renamed Singleton Boulevard in honor of Dallas County Commissioner Vernon Singleton.

[3] Jan I. Fortune, ed., *True Story of Bonnie and Clyde as told by Bonnie's Mother and Clyde's Sister, Mrs. Emma Parker and Mrs. Nell Barrow Cowan* (New York: Signet Books, 1968), 30-32.

[4] John Neal Phillips, *Running with Bonnie and Clyde: The Ten Fast Years of Ralph Fults* (Norman, Oklahoma: University of Oklahoma Press, 1996), 44.

[5] Fortune, 32. Phillips, 45-46. John Ballinger, Texas Hideout (http://www.texashideout.com).

[6] Fortune, 36-41.

[7] Ibid, 43.

[8] Ibid, 47.

[9] W.D. Jones, "Riding with Bonnie and Clyde." *Playboy Magazine*, November 1968, 162.

[10] Blanche Caldwell Barrow and John Neal Phillips, ed. *My Life with Bonnie and Clyde* (Norman, Oklahoma: University of Oklahoma Press, 2004), 25.

[11] Fortune, 49.

[12] Ibid.

[13] Ted Hinton. *Ambush: The Real Story of Bonnie and Clyde* (Dallas: Southwestern Historical Publications, 1979), 7-8, 113-114. Ted Hinton writes that he met Bonnie at the American Café in 1930.

[14] Fortune, 57. In *Bonnie and Clyde: A Twentieth Century Update*, James R. Knight writes that Clyde and his friend, Clarence Clay, visited Buster Parker's (Bonnie's brother) house, where Bonnie and several other people had gathered for some relaxed conversation and visiting (23).

[15] Ibid, 58-67.

[16] Ibid, 69-76.

[17] Along with hardened criminals, Eastham's population consisted of first time offenders, juveniles, and many poor (and mostly black) men who had been caught "loitering," which could earn them a year's sentence. For more on the

decidedly cruel Texas prison system, and subsequent reforms, read *Penology for Profit* by Donald R. Walker.

[18] Phillips, 49-54. John Neal Phillips interviewed Ralph Fults extensively for the book, *Running with Bonnie and Clyde, the Ten Fast Years of Ralph Fults.* Phillips' book is considered the most authoritative on the Barrow gang.

[19] Fortune, 76-78.

[20] Phillips, 54.

[21] Ibid, 65.

[22] Ibid, 49-54.

[23] Phillips' *Running with Bonnie and Clyde* references a bank robbery by the Barrow gang in Lawrence, Kansas that netted them $33,000 during this early gang period. No other historical account has included this robbery.

[24] Other accounts maintain that Raymond Hamilton was instrumental in planning the future Eastham Raid. While Raymond had been reluctant to commit armed robbery, he ended up being the gang member with the most bank jobs to his name, although Clyde was implicated in a good number of them.

[25] Phillips, 75-78.

[26] *Dallas Morning News*, April 21, 1932; Fortune, 81-83. Phillips, 89-101.

[27] *Dallas Morning News*, April 21, 1932.

[28] Phillips, 101.

[29] Caldwell Barrow, 193.

[30] Fortune, 89.

[31] For a great description of this caper, read John Neal Phillips, *Running with Bonnie and Clyde*, 89-101.

[32] Phillips, 74.

[33] Ted Rogers, a one-time member of the Barrow Gang, later bragged about his role in the killing to fellow cell mates. He was never charged with the crime. Raymond Hamilton received the death penalty for Bucher's murder, though he maintained that he was in Michigan at that time.

[34] Clyde's guilt in Howard Hall's murder is still open for debate. The Sherman Police pinned the crime on Clyde Barrow without an investigation. This guilt-by-imagination became a pattern for Clyde. Although he barely committed a third of the crimes he was accused of (though not charged with), he ended up being wanted in several states for robbery and murder.

[35] Fortune, 89.

[36] Lee Simmons, *Assignment Huntsville* (Austin: University of Texas Press, 1957), 128.

[37] Phillips, 160.

[38] Frank Ballinger, Texas Hideout http://texashideout.tripod.com/bc.htm.

[39] Fortune, 107-109.

[40] Ibid, 109-112.

[41] Ibid, 112.

[42] Ibid, 113.

[43] Blanche had always criticized the movie, in which she was depicted as running hysterically into the middle of the melee. In her memoirs, she maintained that she was quite calm. She also wrote that, unlike in the movie, Bonnie never shot at the officers (Caldwell Barrow, 36). W.D. Jones later told interviewers that Bonnie would reload, but would not shoot, though Emma Parker relayed that Bonnie did shoot when needed.

[44] Fortune, 83-85.

[45] Caldwell Barrow, 81-87.

[46] Fortune, 123. Texas State Historical Marker, Collingsworth County.

[47] Ibid, 124.

[48] Ibid, 124.

[49] W.D. Jones Statement, November 16, 1933, Vertical Files, Dallas Public Library. Simmons, 122.

[50] Fortune, 127-128; Caldwell, 110-117.

[51] Phillips, Texas Hideout

[52] Caldwell Barrow, 100-110; Fortune, 131.

[53] Fortune, 129.

[54] Ibid, 132.

[55] Caldwell Barrow, 100-110.

[56] Fortune, 134. Caldwell Barrow, 116-117.

[57] Fortune, 135. Caldwell Barrow, 121.

[58] Fortune, 135.

[59] Fortune, 136-137. Caldwell Barrow, 126-127.

[60] Fortune, 135-142.

[61] *Dallas Morning News*, July 24, 1933. Caldwell Barrow, 133-134.

[62] Caldwell Barrow, 178-179; 184-187. Blanche Barrow Official Site, http://www.blancebarrow.com

[63] W.D. Jones Statement. Phillips, 151.

[64] Fortune, 146.

[65] Ibid, 149-152. Emma Parker relates that the family reunion occurred in Wise County, Texas, but contemporary newspaper accounts locate the failed ambush near Irving, Texas. Since Sheriff Smoot Schmid had no authority in any county but Dallas, one must surmise that Emma Parker was mistaken. Also, other family member related that Clyde did not try to seek revenge for this ambush.

[66] Simmons, 125

[67] Fortune, 155. John Neal Phillips writes that Hilton Bybee was added to the raid by Ralph Fults, not Raymond Hamilton, and Lee Simmons related that Bybee was a "hanger on" and wasn't part of the original escape plan.

[68] According to John Neal Phillips, Joe Palmer had set his sights on Crowson due to a beating he had received by him, though Ted Hinton maintained in his book that Crowson was a decent man. Lee Simmons wrote that Major Crowson's assignment as a mounted guard was to stay well beyond the work detail area so that the prisoners never knew exactly where he was. That

morning, however, Major Crowson rode up to talk to the work detail guards, which ended up costing him his life.

[69] In Fortune's, *The True Story of Bonnie and Clyde*, Emma Parker maintains that Joe Palmer stayed with Bonnie and Clyde up until the Grapevine murders.

[70] Simmons, 166.

[71] Fortune, 158. Many of Mary's more unfortunate characteristics, such as hysterics and loose sexual morals, have been attributed to both Bonnie and Blanche in books and movies.

[72] It was in Houston when Raymond Hamilton wrote a letter disassociating himself from Clyde, which was later posted in the Dallas Time Herald (Fortune, 158). In response, Clyde wrote a scathing letter about Raymond Hamilton to the District Attorney of Dallas, which he mailed from McKinney, Texas (Dallas Morning News, May 23, 1934). Emma Parker and Nell Barrow Cowan doubted that this letter was genuine, though the newspaper claimed a thumb print on the letter matched Barrow's.

[73] Fortune, 160-161.

[74] Fortune, 161. James R. Knight with Jonathan Davis, *Bonnie and Clyde: A Twenty-First Century Update* (Austin: Eakin Press, 2003), 145.

[75] Fortune, 149.

[76] Dallas Morning News, May 24, 1934. Simmons, 128

[77] During this period, Texas law prohibited pursuits across county lines – all law enforcement dealing with crimes beyond their county's jurisdiction would first need special permission to work in another county. Due in part to Clyde's crime spree, Texas changed the law to allow law enforcement more leverage.

[78] *Dallas Morning News*, May 23, 1934. True Story, 162-163.

[79] Fortune, 163. Phillips, 187.

[80] *Bonnie and Clyde Hideout*. Phillips, 193.

[81] Phillips, 192.

[82] *Dallas Morning News*, May 23, 1934. Hinton, 154. Phillips, 193. Fortune, 158.

[83] "Henry Methvin." http://www.tmethvin.com/henry/index.html

[84] Hinton, 158-159. Henry later testified that he purposefully separated from Bonnie and Clyde, which was part of the ambush plan.

[85] Methvin v. Oklahoma (1936)

[86] Oddly, Hamer's account puts this stump/hiding place "eight miles from Plain Dealing, Louisiana," though Plain Dealing is not anywhere in close proximity to Gibsland. Plain Dealing is north of Shreveport, just south of the Arkansas border. John H. Jenkins and H. Gordon Frost. *I'm Frank Hamer: The Life of a Texas Peace Officer* (Austin State House Press, 1968), 222.

[87] Simmons, 133. It is still unclear if Henry Methvin was aware of this plot or not.

[88] Descriptions based on *Running with Bonnie and Clyde* by John Neal Phillips; *Ambush* by Ted Hinton, and *Bonnie and Clyde Hideout* by Frank R. Ballinger.

[89] According to Ted Hinton in *Ambush,* Clyde was not wearing shades because the sun was behind him. However, in photos of Clyde being brought to the coroner after the ambush, his shades dangle from his ears.

[90] Phillips, 310.

[91] Hinton, 169.

[92] Ibid, 170-171.

[93] Fortune, 173-174.

[94] Phillips, 209-210.

[95] Fortune, 173.

[96] Fortune, 170. *Dallas Times Herald,* May 24, 1934.

[97] Texas Hideout; *Dallas Morning News*, May 27, 1934; *Dallas Morning News*, "Hidden History 1926-1950" July 3, 2002.

[98] Fortune, 174-175.

[99] *Dallas Morning News*, May 23, 1934

[100] *Dallas Times Herald*, May 24, 1934

[101] Those are testicles from bulls, deep fried and served with cream gravy. No, I'm not kidding.

Made in the USA
Coppell, TX
10 March 2020

16710074R00075